Also edited by E. O. Parrott

How to Be Well-Versed in Poetry

Compiled and Edited by
E. O. PARROTT

VIKING

VIKING

Published by the Penguin Group
Penguin Books Ltd, 27 Wrights Lane, London W8 5TZ, England
Viking Penguin, a division of Penguin Books USA Inc.,
375 Hudson Street, New York, New York 10014, USA
Penguin Books Australia Ltd, Ringwood, Victoria, Australia
Penguin Books Canada Ltd, 2801 John Street, Markham, Ontario, Canada L3R 1B4
Penguin Books (NZ) Ltd, 182–190 Wairau Road, Auckland 10, New Zealand

Penguin Books Ltd, Registered Offices: Harmondsworth, Middlesex, England

First published in Great Britain by Viking 1990
2 4 6 8 10 9 7 5 3 1

Set in 10/12 pt Lasercomp Garamond
Printed in England by Clays Ltd, St Ives plc

A CIP catalogue record for this book is available from the British Library

ISBN 0–670–82327–9
Library of Congress Catalog Card Number: 90–71286

For all my friends in the Hollyrood Players,
Great Malvern, 1944–6

CONTENTS

INTRODUCTION

This is the fifth book which I have compiled and edited, using material sent in from far and wide by a large but scattered group of writers, most of whom participate regularly in the literary competitions run by the *Spectator*, *New Statesman and Society* and *The Times Educational Supplement*. It is an unusual way of writing a book, and is, so far as I am aware, unique. Anyone who wishes to know how such a system works in practice will find it described in the introduction to our first book *How to Become Ridiculously Well-Read in One Evening*.

When we chose poetry as our topic, it was immediately obvious that examples of the sort of material we submitted to past literary competitions could be included: encapsulations of famous poems, replies from some of the personages, animals and so on, addressed in famous poems, etc. There was a widespread demand for the popular pastime of devising deflationary couplets by adding a second rhyming line to familiar lines of poetry.

The writing of light verse has always featured prominently in literary competitions. Often, the request is that entries should be in the form of a villanelle, a triolet, a rondeau, or one of the many other standard poetic forms.

We thought it would be helpful to include examples of as many of these forms as possible. These would be useful for reference purposes and would also, it was hoped, be of interest to poetry-lovers. Some of the forms are so lengthy that they never occur in literary competitions, but the contributors rose to meet the technical challenge these complex forms presented, and so we have both the rhymed and unrhymed sestina, the five-verse ballade, the rondeau *redoublé*, the pantoum, the chant royal and many others. The lighter forms of verse – limerick, clerihew, double dactyl, ruthless rhyme, etc., have been grouped into a separate section, as have those verses where a count of the number of syllables determines the length of the lines.

It seemed logical to include a section devoted to the various types of stanza found in English poetry. In order to make all this comprehensible, we have included sections dealing with metre, rhyme and a number of the literary terms used in the study of prosody. Finally, I have added a section devoted to rather more specialized verse forms, many of which were devised by the setters of literary competitions to test the patience, ingenuity and skill of any writer foolhardy enough to tackle them. Here will be found an assortment of acrostics, mnemonics, verses using only four-letter words or just one vowel, and other equally esoteric forms of poetry.

Thus, at the heart of this book there is a series of sections which together add up to a kind of layman's introductory guide to English prosody. It may not be as comprehensive or as erudite as more scholarly works on the subject, but we trust it is both comprehensible and entertaining. It may seem to you odd that a book which includes education amongst its aims should also aim to be amusing and, more than that, state that it intends to make you laugh. On reflection, you may think it a pity that more textbooks do not share such aims.

The philosophy of W. S. Gilbert's jester, Jack Point, summarizes our purpose very neatly:

> O winnow all his folly, folly, folly,
> You'll find a grain or two of truth among the chaff . . .

E. O. PARROTT

ACKNOWLEDGEMENTS

I would like to thank all those who have helped me in the compilation of this book: Gavin Ewart, Mike Rees, Edna Smith, John Heath-Stubbs; with a special word of thanks to Beth Bagshaw and, as ever, Tricia, my wife.

Bill Greenwell's 'The Sibilant Soldier' (pages 241–2) was previously published in the *New Statesman*, 1983.

WHY POETRY?

A Poet's Villanelle
(See 'The Villanelle', page 173)

The act of writing verse
  Is singularly hard,
Makes rotten tempers worse,

Incites a man to curse –
  Who wants to be a bard?
The act of writing verse

When no one will disburse,
  Like drawing the wrong card,
Makes rotten tempers worse.

Look at my empty purse!
  Necessity has marred
The act of writing verse;

So, friend, refrain, nor nurse
  Ambition that, ill-starred,
Makes rotten tempers worse,

Nor foolishly immerse
  Yourself – be on your guard!
The act of writing verse
Makes rotten tempers worse.

MARY HOLTBY

On Poetry
(See 'Skeltonic Verse', page 102)

Poetry the pleasure,
The madness, the treasure;
Muse, who can beat her?
Enslave or defeat her?
O rhyming! O metre!
Pathos and passion;
Humour in fashion,
So tripping,
So chiming,
Beyond all explaining,
In meaning
How cunning!
There for the reading,
For counsel and needing,
For borrowing,
Buying,
Laughing and crying,
In all men lies hidden —
Comes flooding unbidden,
Poetry the pleasure,
Madness and treasure.

PHILIP A. NICHOLSON

*

Rhyme Those Blues Away

Writing poetry is a form of auto-therapy
Undertaken by authors when they're feeling off-colour and far from
    cheerful or chirrupy;
Music hath charms to soothe the savage breast,
But verse is an even better way of getting something off your chest;
So when you're plunged in gloom,
Having acquired enough editors' rejection slips to paper the sitting-
    room,

2

Or your ex-wife
Is upsetting your sex life,
Or you're fed up with the telly,
And feel so low you could crawl under a snake's belly,
That's the time
To break into rhyme.
'How to begin?' you ask. Should you take as a model, say, Dante's
    Inferno?
Er – no.
Start with something simpler: a clerihew
(Which was E. C. Bentley's middle name. Oh – you knew?)
Or a limerick – provided that your instinctive prudery
Doesn't stand in the way of the obligatory rudery.
Later, you can progress to something longer, in iambic pentameters,
A favourite metre with amateurs.
('I think, therefore iambic,' as Descartes might have said – in French, of
    course,
Though that would be putting Descartes before the horse.)
How do iambics go? Here's a clue:
'The curfew tolls the knell of parting day.' Got it? And if that's good
    enough for Gray's *Elegy*, it's good enough for you.
By the time you've polished off a few haikus, odes (Pindaric, Sapphic,
    Horatian), sonnets (Shakespearean and Petrarchian), georgics,
    ballads, ballades, rondeaux and rondels, not to mention *bouts-rimés*,
You'll probably be murmuring to yourself, 'What fun! Jolly good
    scheme, eh?'
And if by some unlucky chance you've just been knocked down on a
    zebra crossing (Americans, incidentally, pronounce it 'zeebra'),
And you don't feel like tackling any of the above, you can always fall
    back on *vers libre*.
                    So remember: the poetic Muse
                    Is a sure-fire cure for the blues;
                    A verse a day
                    Keeps the hearse away.

                    STANLEY J. SHARPLESS

Commentary

Now it's the English Language versus
The Poets, and we're all hoping to see
A good clean contest; and it's (yes) . . .Chaucer's
Opening for The Poets – and, Goodness me!

He's got the language, pardee, by the coillons
And twisted it into weird couplets; and now he's passed it
(Yes, he's past it!) and it's gone to Big William
(Captain) who does some beautiful fancy stuff – and he's tossed it

To Abraham Cowley, who's doing his best to hack it
To pieces; but now Milton gets the language: he's loading it with Latin . . .
Meanwhile Pope is fashioning a strait-jacket . . .
Yes . . . the Heroic Couplet – he's got it completely buttoned up, flattened.

But no! English has escaped! It's off again! Dancing! Oh! but it's
        down! in . . .
Yes, it's fallen into a sticky romantic morass –
It struggles free, rallies again, swerves past Tennyson . . . Browning –
Well done! Oh no!! And it's (watch those scissors!) T. S. Eliot to deliver
        the *coup-de-grâce*!

GERARD BENSON

*

Diagnosis

POETRY is . . .
jumping naked into a barrel
of razor-blades,
a distress message from Hell,
acting one's heart out to a sphinx,
gardening in concrete,
an incurable disease.

PHILIP A. NICHOLSON

Prognosis

A POET needs . . .
the optimism of an alchemist,
the gregariousness of a leper,
the patience of Stonehenge,
the stamina of Tarzan,
psychiatry.

PHILIP A. NICHOLSON

*

This Modern Stuff

Modern poetry? I dunno,
    Can't seem to get involved – I try,
attack the stuff with grim resolve,
    but always end up high and dry;
somehow it hasn't any bite,
    for me it's tedious to read
and worse to write;
    myself, I like the crisp and crackly kind
with themes to match
    and rhymes that linger in the mind;
but, then, a man who opens doors for ladies,
    reads Kipling, doesn't swear
and always wears a tie
    is bound to like his poetry square.

PHILIP A. NICHOLSON

TERSE VERSE

Reading poetry is not easy. Many poems are long and most will probably seem longer than they are. The following encapsulations of some of the best-known poems will enable anyone to dispense with the tedious necessity of actually reading the original poems.

*

ANON.

Cuckoo Song

Summer's nigh,
Cuckoos call;
Birdies fly,
Beasties bawl;
Plants grow high,
Creepies crawl;
Clear blue sky,
(I think that's all).

RON RUBIN

6

MATTHEW ARNOLD

Dover Beach

If God's the tide, He's on the turn.
So, baby, let our passion burn.

BILL GREENWELL

*

SIR JOHN BETJEMAN

Slough

Regarding Slough, Berks.,
The poet remarks:
'This town makes me vomit –
I wish they would bomb it!'

RON RUBIN

A Subaltern's Love Song

Feel her foreplay – more than kisses!
Now I'll have to call her Mrs.

BILL GREENWELL

*

RUPERT BROOKE

The Old Rectory, Grantchester

Du Lieber Gott!
I think of Grantchester a lot;
Especially when I have some free time
Around tea-time.

STANLEY J. SHARPLESS

Sonnet: 'If I should die . . .'

Chaps, if I get my chips, please be advised,
The Frog terrain is hereby Anglicized.

MARY HOLTBY

*

ROBERT BROWNING

My Last Duchess

Fond of Art?
She was at heart
I didn't think much
Of my old Dutch.

BILL GREENWELL

The Pied Piper of Hamelin

Rats breed;
Hamelin freed;
Piper not feed;
Kids follow lead.

FIONA PITT-KETHLEY

G. K. CHESTERTON

Lepanto

Don John
Fought on.
Gave Turks
Works.

JOHN STANLEY SWEETMAN

*

SAMUEL TAYLOR COLERIDGE

Kubla Khan

In Xanadu did Kubla Khan
A leisure-complex build,
A Disneyland-cum-Theme-Park
With many wonders filled:
A sacred river, caves of ice,
Even milk of Paradise.
(Clever Kubla, say some scholars,
Had his eye on tourist dollars.)

STANLEY J. SHARPLESS

Old salt
Grabs third.
Tells what
Occurred.
His fault,
'Shot bird,
Saw ghost,
Crew die,
Ship lost,
Not I.'

JOHN STANLEY SWEETMAN

*

DANTE ALIGHIERI

L'Inferno

On Dante's package tour of Hell
The poet Virgil is the guide.
It's cold and no five-star hotel,
But famous names abound inside.

FIONA PITT-KETHLEY

*

WALTER DE LA MARE

The Listeners

Travelled back
On old hack;
Called! Knock, knock!

Got a shock –
Pub is shut –
Empty gut!
    Not a sound, not a cough!
    No one there? Buggered off!

E. O. PARROTT

*

T. S. ELIOT

The Love Song of J. Alfred Prufrock

Life? Ah, what's its gist?
Desist: I'd stick to mist.
Or dream of fishy tryst.

BILL GREENWELL

Rhapsody on a Windy Night

Life at night is quite exciting
Thanks to all this fancy lighting.

BILL GREENWELL

*

EDWARD FITZGERALD

The Rubá'iyát of Omar Khayyam

The poet wonders what life's all about;
The answer, he concludes, is really 'Nowt.'
But with a book, a bird, some bread, some booze,
He figures he'll contrive to stick it out.

PETER VEALE

11

ALLEN GINSBERG

Howl

Disaffected youth
Searches for the Truth:
  via mystic ideas
    & wild panaceas,
    bebop and blues
    & far too much booze,
    homo-erotics
    & lots of narcotics.
The Answer? Despair.
(Life is unfair.)

RON RUBIN

*

THOMAS GRAY

Elegy in a Country Churchyard

Home the cows and cowmen plod;
Evening comes, I'm on my tod
All among the village stiffs,
Brooding over buts and ifs.
Had some disaffected dunce
Verbalized his anguished grunts,
Such a grave would seem too shabby –
He might well have made the Abbey.
I, whom yokels judged *non compos*,
Claim an epitaph more pompous:
Mourn us both, whom Lady Luck's
Left to rot in rural Bucks.

MARY HOLTBY

THOMAS HARDY

The Darkling Thrush

A century begins? I've heard
It get a little bit of bird.

BILL GREENWELL

*

THOMAS HOOD

Bridge of Sighs

Dead bird,
Who erred,
On slab,
Like dab –
Can't face
Rat-race;
Just stares . . .
Who cares?
Tom Hood,
Now, would!

PASCOE POLGLAZE

*

GERARD MANLEY HOPKINS

Hurrahing in Harvest

The sky, the air, the clouds, the breezes!
They make you want to give three cheers for Jesus!

BILL GREENWELL

*

JOHN KEATS

Isabella

Young Isabella loved a fella
Of low degree;
Which, when her brothers saw,
They did deplore;
And did him in, a wicked sin,
As all agree.

Lorenzo's ghost, paler than most,
Returned to tell
His resting-place and, in short space,
Young Isabel
Dug up his head and homeward sped;
She'd wrapped it well.
There she had got a basil-pot
To keep it in.

The basil grew and grew,
Well nourishèd,
Until the evil two, held in abhorrence
By all in Florence,
In guilt had fled.

JOHN STANLEY SWEETMAN

La Belle Dame Sans Merci

'Errant knight, errant knight,
Where have you been?'
'With a girl in a grot,
And that's why I'm so lean.'

FIONA PITT-KETHLEY

Ode on a Grecian Urn

Gods chase
Round vase.
What say?
What play?
Don't know.
Nice, though.

DESMOND SKINNER

On First Looking into Chapman's Homer

Until I came across Chapman,
Homer was a load of crap, man.
Now I think he's terrific,
Like gazing at the Pacific.

STANLEY J. SHARPLESS

To Autumn

Misty fields,
Harvest done,
Gleaners glean,
Mellowing sun,
Apples ripen,
Redbreast tweets,
Favourite season
Of John Keats.

STANLEY J. SHARPLESS

PHILIP LARKIN

Church-Going

In a leaky kirk
I'm your proper, earnest berk!

BILL GREENWELL

The Whitsun Weddings

Carriage-bored, I peep a bit.
Marriage stirs my native whit.

BILL GREENWELL

*

D. H. LAWRENCE

Snake

How amazing, amazing: a snake.

Whack!

Oh, my mistake,
I take it back.

BILL GREENWELL

*

EDWARD LEAR

The Dong with the Luminous Nose

Ever he goes,
Dong with his nose,
   Wandering in sunshine and shade,
All the day long.
Rueful his song:
   'Where is my Jumbly maid?'

Let evening fall, for his
   Efforts seem flat
As a gentleman's call for his
   Runcible cat.

PAUL GRIFFIN

*

HENRY WADSWORTH LONGFELLOW

The Song of Hiawatha

Hiawatha, handsome Injun,
Married girl named Minnehaha,
(Known to friends as Laughing Water).
She died in a dreadful famine,
He walked off into the sunset.
(Very long and rather boring
Narrative in unrhymed trochees:
Tum-ti, tum-ti, tum-ti, tum-ti,
Tum-ti, tum . . . *ad infinitum*.)

STANLEY J. SHARPLESS

*

LOUIS MACNEICE

Bagpipe Music

Life is like a wailing ceilidh
Where they count the money daily.

BILL GREENWELL

*

JOHN MASEFIELD

Sea Fever

Sea beckons,
Lad reckons
　　Needs ship.

Clear day,
Sails away;
　　Long trip.

Comes home,
Writes pome;
　　Has kip.

RON RUBIN

*

JOHN MILTON

L'Allegro

I'm in the mood to be gay
(No, of course, not in *that* sort of way);
To sport in the shade
With a fair willing maid,
I'd be happy for ever and aye.

STANLEY J. SHARPLESS

Il Penseroso

After an amorous session
I feel post-coital depression;
Away, fickle Folly!
Come, sweet Melancholy!
True balm for all such indiscretion.

STANLEY J. SHARPLESS

Paradise Lost

Book I   Satan is from heaven cast,
Book II   Plans from Hell his counter-blast,
Book III   Seeks a human to entice,
Book IV   Spots a pair in Paradise.
Book V   Raphael, sent to blow the whistle,
Book VI   Paints in flashback the dismissal,
Book VII   Tells how God made Man and matter.
Book VIII   Adam and the angel chatter.
Book IX   Satan's apple conquers Eve.
Book X   God invites the pair to leave.
Book XI   Angel Michael clears the garden,
Book XII   Gives a hint of long-term pardon.

NOEL PETTY

Sonnet: 'On his blindness'

'What makes you think,' says Patience, 'God needs *you*.'
'You just wait there till you are spoken to.'

JOYCE JOHNSON

*

ALEXANDER POPE

The Rape of the Lock

Fetishist snips Linda's lock;
The poor gal's in a state of shock,
Until she sees her curls arise
To form a star up in the skies.
'Cor!' she muses. 'How bizarre –
I always longed to be a star!'

RON RUBIN

*

WILLIAM SHAKESPEARE

The Passionate Pilgrim
(*'Crabbed age and youth cannot live together'*)

The young are with it,
The old aren't;
The young can do it,
The old can't.

STANLEY J. SHARPLESS

Sonnet: 'The expense of spirit in a waste of shame'

Bonking is all very well while you're doing it;
The morning after, you find yourself rueing it.

STANLEY J. SHARPLESS

*

PERCY BYSSHE SHELLEY

Ozymandias

A monumental boast, a shattered statue.
Ozzy, the empty desert's laughing at you.

MARY HOLTBY

To a Skylark

Absurd!
You're no bird,
More like a disembodied spirit, really.
Well – nearly.

STANLEY J. SHARPLESS

*

STEVIE SMITH

Not Waving But Drowning

On the brink, or in the drink,
Some (I think) seem in the pink.

BILL GREENWELL

ALFRED, LORD TENNYSON

The Brook

I babble on and on and on,
And on and on and on,
And on and on and on and on,
Just like Lord Tennyson.

STANLEY J. SHARPLESS

Come into the Garden, Maud

Come into yard, Maud,
Wait near gate.
Come into yard, Maud,
Meet your fate.
Grey dawn, soon,
Bats have fled,
Exit moon,
Salt tear shed.
Come fair maid,
Ever been laid?

STANLEY J. SHARPLESS

The Lady of Shalott

Saw knight pass
In glass.
Left room,
Full of gloom.
Stole boat,
Died afloat.

FIONA PITT-KETHLEY

Ulysses

After his travels, Ulysses
Rapidly tired of his missis.
    He said, 'My environs
    Could do with some sirens.
How boring this unalloyed bliss is.'

M. R. MacINTYRE

*

DYLAN THOMAS

Fern Hill

Wake from out my midnight ramble.
Life is just a massive gambol.

BILL GREENWELL

*

WILLIAM WORDSWORTH

Daffodils

I once saw some daffs by a lake,
A wonderful sight – no mistake.
    It gives me a thrill
    To think of them still;
That sure was a real lucky break.

STANLEY J. SHARPLESS

Ode: Intimations of Immortality From Recollections of Early Childhood

To a mite
Things look bright.
Later on
Glory gone.
Still, must say,
I'm OK –
Wise old sort,
Into Thought.

WENDY COPE

The Prelude

Dear Samuel Taylor C.,
Enclosed is some verse. It could be
That there's rather too much
About Nature and such,
But most of it's all about me.

RON RUBIN

The Solitary Reaper

Up hill creeping,
Saw her reaping,
Singing, bending.
Song heart-rending.
What? Cannot say;
But lovely lay!

P. W. R. FOOT

Sonnet: 'Milton! Thou should'st be living at this hour'

England's gone bad, and stinks like rotten Stilton!
She needs a disinfectant such as Milton.

JOYCE JOHNSON

Sonnet: 'The World is too much with us'

We're all too busy haggling in the market.
If Triton blew his conch-shell, who would hark it?

JOYCE JOHNSON

Upon Westminster Bridge

Nice view from here; just stop and look a minute:
Ships, towers, domes, theatres. Pretty, innit?

STANLEY J. SHARPLESS

*

W. B. YEATS

When You Are Old

Every Jack has his Jill,
Every dog has its day;
Now you're over the hill,
And he's far, far away.

RON RUBIN

RIGHT OF REPLY

Poets are notably outspoken in addressing members of the animal and plant kingdoms, not to mention people and even inanimate objects. Here, a few of the addressees of such poems have a chance to answer back.

*

The Birds' Revolt

Swinburne, old Swinburne, silly old Swinburne!
   Sing me no more of that sisterly stuff!
Slink off to the city where women in sin burn;
   Swallows have swallowed enough.
And as for that songbird, which 'Itys' repeats,
It is tired of providing poetical treats,
It is miffed about Milton and curt about Keats,
   And feels it is time to be tough.

For I'll tell you, poor poets, we're all simply sick of
   This maudlin approach to our practical schemes;
You clutch at a straw to make cultural brick of,
   And build a pagoda of dreams,
While all that inspires our spectacular flights
Or the music that moves you on midsummer nights
Is our lust to maintain territorial rights
   With a barrage of bellicose screams.

MARY HOLTBY

*

The Raven's Story

Swaggerin' home in raven fashion, feelin' rather bold and dashin',
Thought I'd do some poet-bashin'; saw this light above a door –
A sign that E. A. Poe was porin' o'er some problem bleak and borin',
Like how to rhyme with Ulalume, or find a maiden named Lenore.
And when I heard the morbid nutter mutter, 'Oh my lost Lenore!'
   I tapped my beak against his door.

Presently the joyless mortal opened up his gloomy portal,
Eyed me with misgiving and inquired what was my visit for.
I said I was a poor old raven, tuckered out and seekin' haven;
Could I rest awhile upon the bust of Pallas o'er his door?
'The bust? Well, if you must,' he answered, clearly shaken to the core,
   'But what news have you of Lenore?'

'By Jeez,' I mused, 'by flamin' golly, this man is clearly off his trolley;
I'll play upon his melancholy as I perch above his door.'
I said: 'Dear Brother Poe, I'm sorry I cannot really ease your worry
Except for some reward which you might bring from your provision store.
A piece of steak would do me nicely – even offal if you're poor.
   Oh, then I might remember more.'

'Corrupt and greedy bird!' he chided. 'Is my sorrow thus derided?
One who's lost a love, as I did, on the Night's Plutonian shore,
Regards your attitude as callous, so please quit the bust of Pallas,
Where you seem quite disposed to stay for half the dreary night or more;
Then pray be good enough to clean the raven-droppings from the floor
   Before you're banished from my door.'

27

I stared him out and wouldn't waver. (Clean up the floor? Do me a favour!)
So finally I got to savour some small offerings from his store.
He fed me, but I kept on stallin'; told him I was past recallin'
Anything of his fair maiden, anything of lost Lenore.
I broke the wretched fellow's spirit with my croaks of 'Nevermore',
    And I'm immortalized for sure.

PETER VEALE

*

The Cuckoo Replies to Mr Wordsworth

O rude old-timer! Thou hast jarred
With thy uneven note.
O William! Shall I call thee bard,
Or but a blundering goat?

In Spring I hear thy plangent bleat
Beside the reedy lake,
And in the fall thy metric feet
Galumphing through the brake.

The shade beneath my chosen tree
Thy fevered muttering fills
As thou pursu'st remorselessly
A rhyme for 'daffodils'.

I hear thee struggling to find
An epithet for me;
Poor poet! I could turn my mind
To multitudes for thee.

NOEL PETTY

*

The Donkey Replies to G. K. Chesterton

All right. You think my head's too big,
And ears are long enough
For wings, but still I don't deserve
This devil's monster stuff.

For you're no picture-plate yourself.
No matter what you do,
You can't be perfect, yet you think
Some kind of God made you.

Old age will dust your hair with grey
And wrinkles line your face,
But I will always look the same
Until I'm called to grace.

And as for that exciting hour
When Jesus rode on me.
I've always borne his symbol on
My back. Didn't you see?

KATIE MALLETT

*

The Horse Responds to the Arab's Farewell

When you released my bridle rein and took the stranger's gold,
I hoped I'd seen the last of you. Oh, not since I was foaled
Had such a surge of happiness run through my horsy heart;
To think that there was every chance that finally we'd part.

It's not that you're a cruel man, you're really very kind:
I've been well fed and stabled too — it would be hard to find
A better billet for a horse; but there's just this, my sheik —
I can't abide your purple prose and all the fuss you make.

I'm quite a simple animal, old penny-plain, that's me,
And the desert's just a desert, not a rolling sandy sea.
Of course I've got some Arab blood, it's that that makes me tick,
Yet 'fleet-limbed' and 'impatient hoof'! You lay it on too thick.

But, Kismet! You have changed your mind and here you go again:
'My beautiful', this 'glossy neck' — why can't you keep it plain?
We've got to make the best of things together, you and I:
If you'll cut down on adjectives, I'll serve you till I die.

JOHN STANLEY SWEETMAN

29

The Tyger's Reply to Blake

Meagre, meagre little man,
Mouth your verses while you can;
Every predator despises
Metaphysical surmises.

Yet I'm forced to ask myself
From what dim and dusty shelf
Did the Source of Being fetch
Such a miserable wretch?

What the pleasure, what the gain?
In what ferment was His brain,
Who after sun and star and cat
Formed so poor a thing as that,

Neither swift nor sage nor good,
Scarcely palatable food?
Yet how impertinently Man
Dares speculate how *I* began!

MARY HOLTBY

*

The Lion Explains

I were sitting there quiet in t' lion 'ouse,
And just thinking as dinner was near,
When a bit of a lad wi' a stick in 'is 'and
Came and poked the thing slap in my ear.

Now this lad were called Albert Ramsbottom,
A nasty and noisy young squirt,
An 'is stick 'ad an 'orse's 'ead 'andle,
But the ferrule were sharp, and it 'urt.

So I did what you might 'ave expected:
I grabbed Albert's mitt wi' both paws,
And dragging 'im quick through the bars of the cage,
I stuffed 'im straight into my jaws.

30

I can tell you 'is flesh were quite tasty,
And I soon 'ad 'im tucked out of sight.
Though 'is parents and all made a terrible fuss,
The Magistrate said I did right.

JOHN STANLEY SWEETMAN

*

The Jaguar's Reply to Ted Hughes

The kids glance and hurry their parents past;
The couples loiter with an abstracted air,
Or pause, like exhausted apes, and stare
At my spots; absorbed in trivia, the trailing host

Of casual strollers files past my cage.
It might be a strange procession or a frieze
Laid on by my keepers between feeds, to ease
My ecstatic boredom or to damp my rage.

But among those who drift in their shoals
Past this prison stands one like a granite block,
Huge, predatory and long-jawed, clutching a book
In which he writes. His dark eyes are spent coals,

His presence a brooding masterpiece of darkness.
The iron bands in his skull bind his brain;
He scours his horizon to determine what I mean
And finds, not me, but his own lurking likeness.

GERARD BENSON

*

The Mouse's Reply to Robert Burns

See what ye've done, you muckle coof,
Wi' your coulter and your nag's great hoof!
Ma hame's all doon from floor to roof.
Oh aye, ye might weel greet,
And stand in dowie self-reproof;
I'm in the mirk and weet!

31

Ye'll sit sae snug in your butt 'n ben,
Guid-willy wi' your dram, and then
Ye'll hae douce thoughts on mice and men
And gowl aboot your duty,
While I'm agley in the cauld, ye ken.
Ye bluidy clootie!

FRANK RICHARDS

muckle = big	guid-willy = cheerful
coof = fool	douce = grave
greet = weep	gowl = howl
dowie = sad	agley = askew
mirk = dark	clootie = devil

*

A Spotted Snake Answers Back

Us spotted snakes wiv double tongue
(I'm tellin' yer) 'ave been took wrong!
That Mustardseed 'ad got the cheek
To say to us the other week –
All la-di-da and 'aughty-like –
'O come not near!' 'Get on yer bike,'
I sez to 'er, 'and don't class *us*
Wiv thorny 'edg'ogs, please, wot wuz
So rahdy yesterday, *nor* newts
Wot splashes all abaht in boots.
And weavin' spiders! Why,' I said,
'We think that they're wrong in the 'ead.
Per'aps you'd arsk yer Pearly Queen
Wot all them goings-on 'as bin!
  But needlin' us poor blokes is steep:
  All *we* want is to get some sleep.'

P. I. FELL

*

32

Cynara Replies to Ernest Dowson

O Ernest, yesternight you frolicked with a tart,
Sampling her coarse bought body as a change from mine.
At what stage was your sweaty lust o'ercome by art?
Did you slip from her side to scribble about *our* passion?
    Well, you certainly got a winner with that line
About being faithful to me, Cynara, in thy fashion.

You've a way with words, my lad; you can make them sing:
'Gone with the wind' posterity could use;
'Wine and roses', too, has a pleasant ring.
Yes, you can turn out verse as smooth as satin;
    But do you need a harlot for your Muse?
And your titles, Ernest – must they be in Latin?

PETER VEALE

*

The Rose Replies to Mr Waller

    Come, precious bard –
Once more thou'd send me forth to woo?
    That old canard
Was worn and weary long ere you,
And dear old Herrick tried it, too.

    Thou bid'st me die
To show how Time relentless flows.
    Let me reply:
Why must it always be a rose
Thou sends't on kamikaze throws?

NOEL PETTY

*

Lucasta Replies to Richard Lovelace

Tell me not, Dick, I should be glad
  You're going to the wars;
Go if you must, I'll not be sad –
  But don't expect applause!

Women must ever wait and weep,
  They say, while men must fight –
There's more to do in bed than sleep
  Through every lonely night.

So don't think that I'll wait for you,
  Chaste as any nun;
You to honour will be true –
  I to having fun!

MARGARET ROGERS

*

The Westron Wynde Replies to Anon.

I'll blowe indede at thy behest,
  The small raine down shall falle.
But as to lovers' armes, and beddes,
  'Tis not my spheare at alle.

Four centuries have gonne, and stille
  Thy curious wordes endure,
Which shows how Man appreciates
  A lewde *non sequitur*.

NOEL PETTY

*

Slough Replies to Sir John Betjeman

Betjeman, I can't see how
You had the nerve to slag off Slough.
We've two lines in the *Blue Guide* now
For industry.

We won a Functionalist award
For tin-sheet roofs, new restored;
They only leaked when it poured
And are rust free.

If you had made a proper search
You would have found one quite old church
With pointy spire and boxy porch
If you'd looked.

We aren't the sorts to moan and groan,
But would you like your worst bits shown
And everywhere be only known
By what you booked?

You did yourself pretty well,
Ringing your anti-Modern bell;
You made your verses sell and sell,
Poet Laureate.

Not wanting to be personal, John,
But that type of Amazon
You fancied, I hope she took you on,
For a date.

REM BEL

35

BORROWED PLUMS

Ogden Nash Rewrites Thomas Gray's 'Elegy in a Country Churchyard'

Sometimes, as I sit here in Stoke Poges Cemetery,
I get to feeling apothegmatory,
And I brood about how some of these humble folks could have been a
    credit to the nation
If only they'd had a high-school education.
This one here, for instance, if he hadn't been cramped in,
Could have been a Hampden;
And that one over there, if he'd been taught the theory and practice of
    making a bomb well,
Might have been a Cromwell.
But taking the long view, I'm inclined to think that the difference
    between being rustic and being Imperial
Is largely immaterial,
Because whether you get a quick man that is born of woman or the full
    military job with cannons going like thunder,
You still finish up six feet under.

NOEL PETTY

William McGonagall Rewrites Percy Bysshe Shelley's 'Ozymandias'

As I was walking out one fine day
Just down by the glorious bridge of Tay,
I met a man who said he'd travelled far and wide,
And on his way a wondrous statue he'd espied.

There were two legs of stone, or so he said,
And beside them there lay a great and broken head,
But he did not say if it had any hands
On whether any arms lay on those golden sands.

He said the face was frowning, as well it may,
Lying in the sand the live-long day,
Though maybe it was the way the ancient sculptor saw
The model for his statue in those long lost years of yore.

Underneath the legs was some writing, and there he read
About a fellow Ozymandias, who was evidently dead,
Who used to be the King in that dry country.
(For I gather it was a fearful way from the sea.)

The writing also said he should look around
To see what the King had made, but nothing there was found
Except for a lot of sand, which stretched for miles away,
With never a sign of water, not even the River Tay.

KATIE MALLETT

*

Dylan Thomas rewrites William Wordsworth's 'Daffodils'

Now as I was young and easy under the lonely clouds,
Green as the lilting valleys and high as the lolling hills,
    The floor beneath the forest dancing,
        Time led me to a dell
      Golden with the trumpets of bright flowers.
(Now, gentry among peasants, I am bard of the happy town
Of Ambleside by Grasmere; then, at holy, childlike will
        I wandered nature's plantings
      By the footpaths where dear Lucy dwelt.)

And as those daffodils fluttered, continuous as the stars
Paving immortal paths and singing in the lucid night
     (In the night that is death once only),
         Time let me stand and see
     Vibrant thousands lovely at my feet.
Agaze and gulping, I was poet and prophet, the waves
Roared in my ears, the pilgrim in my head ran reeling wild,
     As once when a solemn cliff told me
         It would haunt my dreams.

All the lake long they were dancing, they were singing, their pealed
Tunes soaring like larks high over cow byres, long lovely hours
     Of psalming both jocund and joyful.
         I grew gay as they,
     And sprightly too, gyrating in that dale,
Though little I thought that forever my fate was sealing;
That all life long I'd hear, resting on couches, those faint sounds
     Ringing soft in my head, uncloying,
         Lambent with brave praise.

Never I knew, in those passionate days, time would trap me
Writing sonnets on church history and automatic odes
     On the death of some viscount's sister
         While that special scene,
     Flowers and lake, dwindled, and after sleep
I'd wake to a life forever fed by the GPO.
Oh as I was young and daffodils were dancing on the green,
     A pompous, dull, old, inward mister
         Plotted time's treachery.

TOM AITKEN

*

T. S. Eliot Rewrites Alfred, Lord Tennyson's 'The Charge of the Light Brigade'

Let us go, then, since we have had the call
And the guns stretch out before us,
Like salt pots on certain restaurant tables,
And smells of onions linger in the tent-flaps
And sawdust is spilled on the grass;
Let us go into this valley,
This valley of broken stars
Where we must bend the knee
And where an unseen figure bids us on . . .

'You can go but be back soon.'
'All right, Jack. Be seeing you.'
'You will hurry, won't you?
There's not much time.'

Between the spoken message
And the message heard,
Between the going on
And the coming back
Falls the responsibility.
            We'd rather you made no reply

Between the explosion
And the sabre cut,
Between the cannon on the right
And those on the left
Lies the danger.
            Sorry, there's been a mix-up

Then spoke the thunder
DA
Datta: what have we done?

N. J. WARBURTON

*

39

Gerard Manley Hopkins, in a Very Private Moment, Rewrites John Donne's 'The Sunne Rising'

I caught this morning's poke-nose peep-
er through curtained windows, finger-wag schoolmaster in his chiding
Of the romping, arching, underneath-each-other lovers. Hiding
Deep here, how we sport (after breast-clutched, leg-winding sleep)
In our ecstasy! But no, in comes old creep-
light, droning of day and night and WORK, officiously siding
With those who would sunder us. My heart deriding
Cried out, defiant. Busy old fool! Go, take a long leap!

Push off! And bother and pry, oh, badger, somewhere
Else! Dustmen, paperboys, monks, a million
Need your wake-up harshness, not we. This bed – yes, attend here! –

Bounds the wimpling world. Warm us; you warm the Castillian,
The Indian, all. But, best depart, my dear.
What we do next will make you blush vermilion.

TOM AITKEN

*

Hilaire Belloc Rewrites William Wordsworth's 'Michael'

Michael (and Isabel, his wife)
Were far too prone from early life
To put their Trust in human kind.
When Providence, to Virtue blind,
Served up a bill they couldn't pay
They sent son Luke to Save the Day.
Young Luke, who'd rather Had his Fill
Of tending sheep on Greenhead Ghyll,
Just wandered off beyond recall
To be the Blackest Sheep of all.
So Michael died, his Helpmate too:
It seemed the Decent Thing To Do.

NOEL PETTY

W. H. Auden Rewrites John Keats's 'Ode on a Grecian Urn'

This is a nice vase that's so very Greek;
It's plenty to say although it can't speak.

Some figures play pipes, while some play the drum;
Whatever the music, forever they're dumb.

Some men are hunters, the women pursuing;
I cannot but wonder what they are doing.

Their love is lasting, unlike us poor quick;
When real passion ends, it makes people sick.

On this side of the jar, a priest takes a bow;
Are those people watching him killing a cow?

Did they come from that city and leave its streets dead?
Their secret's still secret, for nothing is said.

This Hellenic pot's a permanent token,
Outlasting the living, unless it is broken.

Its splendour will live; that's true, you'll agree;
Thus, truth equals beauty; that's proved. QED.

E. O. PARROTT

*

Geoffrey Chaucer Rewrites Philip Larkin's 'Toad'

TODES

A clerk of Oxenford and eke of Hulle
Was pleyning, 'I have hadde a bely-fulle
Of swinken: like a todes poyson, werk
Soileth my sowle, maketh my lightnesse derk;
That I moot doon, for payen bed and bord,
Six dayes swink is nat of fair accord.
Why sholde nat I with pickfork smite this beeste
Aweye – I sholde nat sterven atte leeste,

41

Sin otheres withouten bisinesse
Live by hir wits in gladsom recchelnesse?
Wolde I coude telle myn maysters what to doon
With hir fool werk, maugre myn pensioun.
Allas! my sowle a tode-lyke melancholy
Y-coupleth with myn lust for leyser joly!'

MARGARET ROGERS

*

Rudyard Kipling Rewrites John Keats's 'La Belle Dame Sans Merci'

'Do up your buttons, Atkins, T.,
    An' put your 'elmet on your 'ead.
What ails you, lad? By Gawd, you look
    At least 'arf dead.

'Your chums in barracks are asleep;
    It's hours since bugles blew last post,
So why are you a-wanderin' 'ere
    Like some damned ghost?

''Ave you bin swiggin' native booze
    Or 'as the sun burnt out your brain?
Per'aps some 'ore 'as wrecked your 'ealth?
    You'd best explain.'

'Well, sarge, I met this bit o' skirt
    (Or bit o' sari, should I say?);
The best I've come acrost, I swear,
    Since Mandalay.

'She took me to a little room
    Somewhere be'ind the old bazaar.
She poured me drink an' played real sweet
    On 'er sitar.

'Then passion, like it does, took 'old;
    We romped in bed hour after hour.
I fell asleep, an' in my dreams
    It all turned sour.

42

'I saw old chums I knew 'ad died,
      An' 'eard a doleful voice declare:
"That girl's the Bell Darm Song Mercee –
      Tommy, beware!"

'I woke, but I was in a daze;
      Some drug 'ad set me 'ead awhirl.
Me money an' me watch 'ad gone –
      An' so'd the girl.'

'Atkins, you're just a bloomin' fool;
      That little lesson cost you dear.
Better go sick – in case she's left
      A souvenir.'

PETER VEALE

*

Don Marquis Rewrites Thomas Gray's 'On a Favourite Cat Drowned in a Bowl of Goldfish'

mehitabel says
a friend selima
a pretty stupid cat
by all accounts
balanced her tabby body
on the edge of a
chinese porcelain
goldfish bowl and
fell in and after coming up
eight times expired
this caused some distress
to the human who thought
she belonged to him
who fantasized about a maid
reaching for gold
and as everybody knows
there is nothing like loot
to get a dame

43

going over the top
if not actually
falling but
what the heck

a fish is only a fish
even if it looks gold
it is not gold *per se*
but refracted light
through scales
and once you ve fallen
like a beetle on its back
you re pretty well stuck
with your position
and no one yet
has undone time
not even old doc einstein
i know about this
because i am an
educated cockroach
                    archy

KATIE MALLETT

*

William Blake Rewrites T. S. Eliot's 'The Hollow Men'

A Scarecrow with his Head of Straw
Is fill'd with Nothing evermore.
The Blind Man's dreams are full at Night
Of those in Heaven still with Sight.
The Dullard wakening to Despair
Has Thoughts compos'd of empty Air.
The Fools that by a Cactus pray
Shall never kiss at break of Day.
The crowd upon the hopeless Beach
See Rose & Star they ne'er can reach.
He who hears the Five Bells chime
Shall chant a final Nursery Rhyme.

A Shadow falling here & there
Defeats Man's Memory of Prayer.
A quiet not a violent Noise
Proves the End of this World's Joyes.

BILL GREENWELL

*

Philip Larkin Rewrites W. B. Yeats's 'The Second Coming'

That falcon up there with still wings
Has got right away from its boss.
No one can tidy up things.
The world's an anarchic mess.

The yobboes are seized by blood lust.
It's the innocents who will die.
The best are wimps, while the worst
Get nastier every day.

I'd like to imagine that God,
Or some such, will sort it all out.
A Second Coming? Oh, sod!
Something's gone wrong with my sight.

I'm surrounded by miles of sand.
It's not the beach at Hull.
There's a shape with the head of a man,
But it looks like a lion as well.

Its gaze is blank but displeased.
It's moving – but only its thighs.
Some vultures, indignant, seem teased.
It's gone now. I hope it stays.

Was that about anything? Well,
Since Jesus popped down for his visit
We've had two thousand years of hell.
Was my dream a portent? God, is it?

TOM AITKEN

COMING TO TERMS

An aspect of poetry that baffles many laymen is the jargon. In this section some of the commonest terms are explained.

*

ALLITERATION

Some writers rate readers as rotten and ratty
And treat them to tricks that are terribly tatty.
Alliteration attempts to achieve,
By beating the bleeders until they believe,
Or glibly and gushingly giving them grounds,
Since they see such a sequence of similar sounds,
For taking the tale they are telling as true
And accepting the author without more ado.

Does it work? Well, it won't when the wise are awake;
But they sink to sleep sometimes, for sanity's sake,
And then the tendentious all talk of technique
And the poorest of poets is praised to the peak.

Lady Luck, labour lovingly: leave me alive;
Send the sages to sleep! So, my song may survive.

PAUL GRIFFIN

More Thoughts on Alliteration

Plenty of poets in past ages
Were anxious to achieve alliterative measures;
Rhyme was too rigid for their romances,
Being strict and strangling, like a strait-jacket.
They listened lovingly to William Langland
Proclaiming passionately his *Piers Plowman*,
Then went and wove three words in each line
That started suitably with the same letter.

Practice is paramount in all poetry;
Convention gives colour and causes acceptance.
It was lousy luck for these lonely labourers
That Chaucer chose to champion rhyme.
They were just journeymen; he was a genius.
He tore them to tatters in his *Canterbury Tales*,
With their rim-ram-ruff and their rant and roarings;
And authors afterwards for all ages
Made a model of that marvellous man.

I wonder whether, without his wisdom,
I'd be doing my damn'dest to describe to readers
The reason why rhyme was regarded as rubbish
After the awfulness of the Middle Ages.

PAUL GRIFFIN

*

BATHOS

When purple passion grabs you by the scruff,
   You'll find the world entirely sympathetic,
So swear eternal love, and all that stuff,
   And settle down to savour the bathetic.
Love is a pretty powerful emotion
   Which lasts for ages when you find you're caught;
It's like a lighthouse when you're on the ocean
   That shines to guide you safely into port.
Once there, of course you'll need a change; be fair –
   You can't go on for years with anyone;
And girls grow old, and lads acquire grey hair.
   With someone younger you can have more fun.
     Oh, love will last quite long, I think you'll find,
     Until the day it gets to be a bind.

PAUL GRIFFIN

*

CENTO, OR POETIC CONSEQUENCES

Souls of poets dead and gone,
What Elysium have ye known?
John Keats

One of the things departed poets get up to (writes our Elysian Correspondent) is playing Poetic Consequences. Each player contributes a line, folds over the paper and passes it on to the next person, who does the same, and so on. A typical result is appended.

When lovely woman stoops to folly [Goldsmith]
In the happy fields of hay, [Housman]
Then heigh-ho, the holly, this life is most jolly,[Shakespeare]
Gather ye rosebuds while ye may. [Herrick]

My heart leaps up when I behold [Wordsworth]
Thy long-preserved virginity, [Marvell]
Bring me my arrows of desire, [Blake]
Because my love has come to me. [Christina Rossetti]
Let us go then, you and I, [T. S. Eliot]
Under the wide and starry sky, [R. L. Stevenson]
We'll tak' a cup o' kindness yet, [Burns]
Lest we forget, lest we forget. [Kipling]

Of course, you don't have to be famous, or dead, to play this game yourself. Take any well-known lines from different poets and string them together. For instance, combining Keats, Landor and Tennyson, you might come up with something like this:

> Much have I travelled in the realms of gold,
> Nature I loved, and next to Nature, Art,
> And slowly answered Arthur from the barge,
> 'It sinks, and I am ready to depart.'

STANLEY J. SHARPLESS

Proposal in Cento

So we'll go no more a-roving so late into the night. [Byron]
I will make you brooches and toys for your delight. [R. L. Stevenson]
Come live with me and be my love, under the greenwood tree.
    [Donne/Shakespeare]
By the old Moulmein pagoda, in that kingdom by the sea. [Kipling/Poe]

FRANK RICHARDS

*

CHAIN VERSE

I had to write a verse, but it was clear
I had few words to use; to ease my plight
I made a chain.

I made a chain of words, as you can hear
The last phrase links the stanzas, as I write
The method's plain.

The method's plain to see; two stanzas share
The rhymes I chose to use, but with the third
The sounds are changed.

The sounds are changed; alas, with few to spare
I have to stop before the final word
Is re-arranged.

KATIE MALLETT

*

THE CONCEIT

When poets speak of their 'conceit',
It's not of arrogance they speak
But some outrageous, cunning feat
Of metaphor, a mite oblique,
As 'Love is like a Rubik Cube'
Or 'Sex is like a Ricicle'
Or 'Marriage is a toothpaste-tube'
Or 'Death is like a bicycle' –
And these they prove in twisty style
By turning logic inside out.
Conceit is literary guile
(But also arrogance, no doubt).

BILL GREENWELL

*

THE CONCRETE POEM

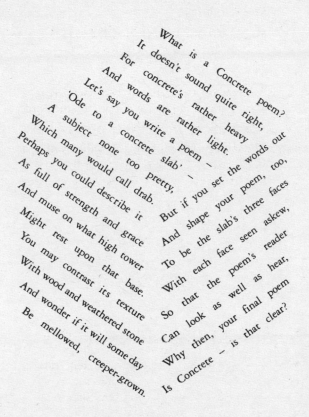

What is a Concrete poem?
It doesn't sound quite right,
For concrete's rather heavy
And words are rather light.
Let's say you write a poem –
'Ode to a concrete slab' –
A subject none too pretty,
Which many would call drab.
Perhaps you could describe it
As full of strength and grace
And muse on what high tower
Might rest upon that base.
You may contrast its texture
With wood and weathered stone
And wonder if it will some day
Be mellowed, creeper-grown.
But if you set the words out
And shape your poem, too,
To be the slab's three faces
With each face seen askew,
So that the poem's reader
Can look as well as hear,
Why then, your final poem
Is Concrete – is that clear?

NOEL PETTY

51

SHOULD SOME MADMAN
PRESS THE BUTTON AND THE
DREADFUL SIRENS SOUND, I SHALL
LIKE MANY OTHERS SEEK A REFUGE
UNDERGROUND, BUT NOT IN ANY BUNKER
OR SUBTERRANEAN TOMB – I'LL PASS MY FINAL
HOURS BEFORE INEVITABLE DOOM IN MY
COMFORTABLE CELLAR STOCKED WITH
MEMORABLE WINE – THERE IN ROMAN
FASHION

I'LL

LANGOROUSLY

RECLINE,

DRINK

THE DIONYSIAC SPRINGS

COMPLETELY DRY, THEN QUIETLY DIE.

PHILIP A. NICHOLSON

Concrete Cat

I?   I
get   out
of bed   and go
to where   the tea
and milk   are kept,
The dishes are post-prandial, the floor has not been swept,
While Jane de l'Aga and Gandy Puss and cute wee Orange Fluff
Lie on *The Times*, or in a carton, like people sleeping rough,
(ha! ha!). The stove is warming them, they're being gently stewed;
Two slits appear in each turned head, their eyelids, badly glued,
Soon fall right apart, pupils shrink from a small ball-bearing size,
To edge-of-blade dimensions, and now shine their green-and-yellow eyes.
Like eagles who spy their prey and dive off a windy, craggy ridge,
They jump to the floor and trot to the vicinity of a potentially opening fridge.
I pick up the tin-opener, and this action drives them wild,
As their close cousin, the tigress, becomes maddened if you molest her only child.
Then they contort themselves for their on-going wash.
And you're off to work to get the wherewithal for Kitty Treats and Whiskas Rogan Josh.
To curl, recurl, then exercise by curling up again
Would keep us flexi-backed, sensuous and sane.
But that's not for the poor likes of us,
While Jane de l'Aga and Gandy Puss
Surely know their stuff,
as does Orange Fluff.

REM BEL

53

DIDACTIC OR 'USEFUL' VERSE

Verse has often been used to communicate information, Virgil's *Georgics* being one famous example. Here are two shorter ones.

Poor Knights' Pudding (*a Haiku*)

Bits of wine-soaked bread
Dipped in beaten egg and fried.
Add cream and sugar.

E. O. PARROTT

Connection Direction
(*Wiring a Plug*)

Up there in green and yellow stripe
Lurks 'E', a downright *earthy* type,
Below him, cool in palest blue,
Lives 'N', a *neutral* through and through,
While opposite in sober brown
Sits 'L', the *liveliest* lad in town.

PHILIP A. NICHOLSON

*

First trawl the sea of life to find a cause,
A subject worthy of your pen's applause,
Then choose the shell, the metre and the style
To hold your pearl, as patient Muses smile.
Thus write a poem, choosing words with care
Until you have a polished gem to share.
And if you have some knowledge to impart,
Present it ribboned round with verbal art –
An ancient form of teaching and a tactic
To bring a lesson home, that's verse didactic.

KATIE MALLETT

*

THE EPITHALAMION

A Poem for a Marriage
(For George MacBeth and Penny Church)

The epithalamia are so many!
(Though
when I was married, I didn't have any.)
Thousands! And so
I'm a little shy of adding to the score –
perhaps the Muse won't want to hear any more?

But George is a very classical person;
he
won't mind if I voice or verse an
elegant wee
Anglo-Scottish odd kind of ode –
it's a way of sending love and good wishes in code.

And most surely the Muse must like Penny?
and,
from Aberdeen to Abergavenny,

know that the hand
best suited to be taken in marriage
is hers? So I retract my undercarriage

and take off boldly! The empyrean
seems
full of Byronic-Assyrian
erotic dreams –
I'm sure they'll live there happily!
Blissful as the *lazzaroni** in Napoli!

*The *lazzaroni* (criminal layabouts) of Naples are
traditionally supposed to lead a carefree and un-
trammelled existence.

GAVIN EWART

*

EUPHONY

Sweet euphony: a melody in sounds,
Voluptuously, sensuously, breathes low
In flowing vowels' ample spread and slow
Silk-padded consonants that cradle round;

Slips down the throat like honeyed syllabub,
Weaves cobweb's lace upon the day's deep dreams.
Cacophony's tin-rattle cat-clawed screams
Bully and batter, make a shrill hubbub.

D. A. PRINCE

*

HYPERBOLE

Exaggeration – that's hyperbole,
In prose, in poetry and verbally.
'Over the moon', or 'old as the hills'?
Impossibilities: both over-kills.
Emphasis clings to its dosage of hype –
Never let on that hyperbole's tripe.

D. A. PRINCE

*

MACARONIC VERSE

A pedant recently averred
In accents short and tense,
'I don't believe you've ever *heard*
Of macaronic verse!'

I shook my head. 'O tempora,'
I cried, 'O mores, too!
And further, 'Qué sera sera!
Peccavi! Taisez-vous!'

T. L. McCARTHY

*

METAPHYSICAL POETRY

I wonder by my troth how they could write
    The sort of verse I purpose to design;
Once poets made this sort of stuff all night.
    In Jacobean times, and Caroline;
They called it Metaphysical; our day
    Hates science, I suppose,
And finds new forms for what it wants to say
    Or puts its complicated thoughts in prose;
But once poets loved this way.

Go catch a falling star . . . but stars don't fall . . .
    Except for meteorites. Perhaps they'll do
To show how love, an incandescent ball
    Falling like Lucifer from me to you,
Ruins my world in one immense explosion,
    Bearing upon its winds
Illimitable hints of joy ambrosian
    That subtly upon human hearts and minds
Work damage by erosion.

These fancy metres, this informal feel,
    The scientific image, none too nice,
Make up the Metaphysical appeal,
    Grabbing you like a metal-worker's vice
That holds and drills and trims until you're free
    To join the great machine
And be the cog that you're ordained to be,
    Whatever shapeless lump you once have been
In God's cosmology.

And yet I've noticed this preordination
    Falls very commonly beneath one head:
The female reader, full of trepidation,
    Finds she is summoned to the poet's bed.
In times when poetry commands no fee
    There must be *some* reward;
So come, be Metaphysical with me,
    My dear Corinna, for I can't afford
To write this stuff for free.

PAUL GRIFFIN

*

ONOMATOPOEIA

I

Onomatopoeic words
May come when one's describing birds:
The coughing bass of crows that croak
Like bronchial vagrants hoicking smoke;
The wooing pigeons in the gloom,
Whose gurgles undulate and boom;
A blackbird in a nervous state,
Metallic as a rusty gate;
Slick sparrows fluttering round the ricks
Or sitting chattering in the sticks.
The sense, you see, is helped by sound.

In Milton proper names abound
That subtly second all he writes:
Those British and Armoric knights,
Involved, it seems, in nasty fights,
Gain dignity, as scufflers can,
By being based in Montalban.

Some novelists also seem to use
The onomatopoeic ruse.
I think they choose their names, for ease,
From telephone directories –
Like Mutimer and Gravenell,
Ellender, Juling, Ingamell –
For their more dignified of tales;
But when their well of patience fails
And they see life's grotesqueries,
Their characters are named like these:
Armbruster, Darkin, Brundish, Futter,
Weatherhog, Remblance, Steggles, Rutter.
The whole of life is seen among
The surnames of our English tongue.

So I shall send, in poetry,
Two placid men to sail the sea,
While zephyrs puff the summer air
And warmth and peace are everywhere.
Come, Windebank and Uffendale,
Sweetly control the flapping sail
And float my gentle verse like this
In onomatopoeic bliss.

PAUL GRIFFIN

*

PARODY

The Golden Road
(after J. E. Flecker)

We who with verse beguile your pilgrimage
    And mock great poets with our hollow pen
May well be called the vampires of our age.
    Sucking the blood from greater, wiser men.

We are the parodists, master; we must paste
    Always a little further; it may be
Beyond that mountain that is still called taste,
    Across the borders of propriety.

Sweet to ride forth in Flecker's style, and try
    Partly to make you smile, and partly see
The sort of opportunities that lie
    Along the Golden Road of Parody.

If we have done our work the way we need,
    The talk of veils and caravans that's heard
May show the Oriental style's indeed
    A High Romantic dream that's half absurd:

The talk of magic, and peculiar vice,
  The isles, the ivory, the palm-girt wells,
The bales of broideries, and sacks of spice,
  The prophets, and the melons, and the bells.

This from a boy who went to Uppingham,
  Took a degree at Cambridge with the best,
Then died because he did not give a damn
  How cold the sea was in the Middle East.

A boy who loved an image in his mind
  And made us see it too; so, though we mock
The way he wrote, we cannot but be kind,
  For we are half in love with poppycock.

And when the darkness falls on our delight,
  We sleep, with Flecker, by the moonlit sea,
Dreaming another journey through the night
  Upon the Golden Road of Parody.

PAUL GRIFFIN

'In the Manner of . . .'

We are the poets who by choice
Eschew the individual voice,
The parodists, the pastiche-makers,
The copyists, the honest fakers.
We take a published verse and bend
Its purpose to a different end;
We have our sport, but come the day
That minor talent slips away
Or ever-lurking Father Time
Draws the blind on life and rhyme,
They'll look upon our works and say
'Another's labours smoothed his way.'

PHILIP A. NICHOLSON

*

61

SIMILE

Fat Feet

I'm tired as a toffee
and sweating like a sweet —
who knows, in verse or prose,
the true fatness of my feet?

I'm sorry as a sawmill
that I walked from Crew to Crete!
Lord knows, my poor old toes
are fatigued by my fat feet!

I want to bellow like a bull,
to bay or baa or bleat!
Like those big black crows
Cry out *Cor*! for my fat feet!

GAVIN EWART

*

SPRUNG RHYTHM

Gerard Manley Hopkins developed this from his study of the alliterative verse of the early English poets. He used devices such as archaic vocabulary, Anglo-Saxon words and inversion of phraseology, to achieve what he called an 'abruptness' in the line, with one strong accent on every metrical foot. The caesura (see page 77) is often used to form part of the foot, just as if it were a word.

As the dare-earth mole snuffles downward in soft soil
    Working for worms, so for life's losses, all
That goes bad, wild, weak, I seek, dazed with coil,
    And by the name Sprung Rhythm these crazed ways call.

Hard hoeing this to thee I dare swear, if in doom
  Lies deep that which I, lost in words and worms, crave;
Oh, if in tumbled, jumbled language, gleeful in gloom
  I tend ever to man's end (grateful or nay), the grave.

Yet freshed I feel, like fox freed from his tiresome trail
  As to wanhope I wend. And if to comprehend
Is hard, so dense my tense, my scansion brimmed with bale:
  Ah me! 'Tis ever so, my frail, my feeble friend.
To clock such cobblers see you then easier means?
Mouth any such, my master, to the (ha! ha!) Marines.

PAUL GRIFFIN

*

READING THE METRE

FEET

1

Homer, consulting a work, put it back, till a
Foot re-emerged where the binding was cracked, till a
Voice issued forth from the foot: 'I'm a DACTYL, a
Dactyl, a dactyl, a dactyl, a . . .
                              (*fades out in the distance*)

2

Is it North? Is it South? Is it West? Is it East
    That this foot is desiring to go?
Mr Parrott, permit me present ANAPAEST
    As she slithers and slips in the snow.

Who speaks? One speaks. Qui dit? On dit.
Hob-nail-boot feet. Tread firm, SPONDEE.

You that dance the hokey-cokey –
Foot, what's *your* name? Me, sir? TROCHEE.

A *common* sort of foot, I am –
   My blood-group would be 'O':
Iamb I am, Iamb I am,
    IAMB. So now you know.

P. I. FELL

*

SPONDEE

Milk-cart

Slow sleet, still street; far beat huge feet;
Clip-clop, start-stop, ear-flop, turd-drop;
Pint-take, gate-shake, sleep-break, house-wake;
Short stay; stamp, neigh; on way – new day.

MARY HOLTBY

*

AMPHIBRACHIC METRE

The Amphibrach in Latin we are taught
Has quantities expressed thus: short – long – short.
In English prosody this kind of foot
Three syllables contains, with accent put
Upon the middle one, as in excited,
Departure, or extinguish or delighted.

Example: Some Horrible flaming reporter
Has loathsomely libelled my innocent daughter.
'Twould give me, I tell you, unlimited pleasure
To strangle the scurrilous swine at my leisure;
To watch him expiring would be, you'd agree, a
Great joy; with his newsprint stuffed down his trachea.

W. F. N. WATSON

*

CHORIAMBICS

As some faltering yacht, spinnaker set, checks to a failing wind,
So I, wondering why, come to a stop, find choriambics hard.
Till now, I hadn't a care, scribbling on; happy I was to write
Verse born deep in the heart, nourished by time, English above all else:
Blank verse, sonnets and odes; syllable strong, syllable weak, in turn.
No strange Roman ideas, rigidly held, all about length of sounds
Stirred my Muse into verse certain to cause torture to all who heard.
Straight sense tells me to turn classical rules into an English form.
Which done, here is the wind, full in my sails: off I can fare at last.

PAUL GRIFFIN

*

THIRD ASCLEPIAD

Third Asclepiad starts like this – a metre from Lesbos isle.
'James James Morrison Morrison' got very near its style.
Though it's not easy to write, nevertheless, old mate,
    Let's try bringing it up to date.

Prince Charles said to his Mother, though she was only Queen:
'I'd be good if the architects would, but that's what they *haven't* been!'
– Blew gaps in the architect chaps wide as the Yorkshire Dales
    (Prince Charles, known as the Prince of Wales).

Prince Charles heard from his Mother: 'Charlie,' she said, said she,
'If you *must* make hay of the RIBA you should clear it with Mrs T.
To my distress the whole of the Press are humming like angry bees.
    Prince Charles, try to be kinder, *please*!'

Prince Charles said very little after his Mother spoke:
Some say he waits for the day, some that his heart is broke;
To my mind he's trying to be kind when architects lose their nerve –
    Far, far kinder than they deserve!

PAUL GRIFFIN

*

Happy Feet

    Dimeters per line have TWO feet,
    Trimeters, they have THREE;
    Tetrameters have FOUR to meet,
    Pentameters, FIVE; see?
    Hexameters have SIX complete –
    Enough for you and me!

    'Examples, please,' I hear you ask;
    Well, here are just a few
    To start you off upon the task –
    The rest is up to you.

W. F. N. WATSON

MONOMETER

Somehow monometer was omitted from our little introductory verse, 'Happy Feet', but it doesn't take a classical education to work out what is meant by the term.

IAMBIC

The Angler's Lament

I wish
The fish
Would bite
To-night.
It's mad.
I've had
Enough.
It's tough.
I freeze.
I sneeze.
My bum
Is numb.
I'll quit
And sit
No more.

Before
They close
At Joe's
Fish shop,
I'll stop
And try
To buy
Some hake
To take
And fry.

Good-bye.

FRANK RICHARDS

TROCHAIC

Wicked
Baron
Took our
Karen
In his
Carriage,
Promised
Marriage,
But just
Laid her
And be-
trayed her;
Now cor
lummee –
Unwed
Mummy.

W. F. N. WATSON

ANAPAESTIC

Mary Rose,
So they say,
Calls her nose
Retroussé;

But a chap
In the pub
Said: 'What crap!
It's just snub.'

W. F. N. WATSON

DACTYLIC

Gnus in Brief

Up jumped a
Wildebeeste;
Piet said: 'We
Killdebeeste.'
Mit lead he
Filldebeeste;
Teatime we
Grilldebeeste.

W. F. N. WATSON

AMPHIBRACHIC

Our darling
Miss Mabel
Drinks Carling
Black Label,
Exalting
Perception
But halting
Conception.

W. F. N. WATSON

*

DIMETER

TROCHAIC

Damn the Huns and
Goths and Lombards;
Damn the monk who
First made bombards:
Ancient hist'ry
So unruly
Is a Myst'ry
To yours truly.

W. F. N. WATSON

AMPHIBRACHIC

Pun and Games

A practical joking
Old-time quack physician
In manner provoking
Abused his position.

While bleeding a humble
Bargee's busty daughters
He started to fumble
Around their hindquarters.

They thought him just flirting
By flexing the muscles,
But he was inserting
A leech in their bustles.

W. F. N. WATSON

*

TRIMETER

TROCHAIC

Hia What-ho

See the little redskin
Wiv 'is bow an' arrer,
Creepin' rahnd 'is wigwam
For to shoot a sparrer.

W. F. N. WATSON

IAMBIC

The lady with the lamp
Went round the ward one night,
And there a vulgar scamp
Gave her a fearful fright.

W. F. N. WATSON

DACTYLIC

Polly, you're quite unappeasable!
Twice in one morning's not feasible!
How can we act so indecently
When we've just done it so recently?
And to each passer-by locally,
Giving the game away vocally
Plain to be seen 'mid the greenery,
Nicking the plums from the deanery.

W. F. N. WATSON

*

TETRAMETER

ANAPAESTIC

It's the pace of a race, it's the grace of the chase,
It's the beat of the feet of a horse on the course;
It is found in the bound of a hound on the ground . . .
Like the toll of a bell for the knell of a soul
Or the roll of a ball down the fall of a fell,
Like a throb of the heart, like the sob when we part,
Like the groan when we moan, like the laugh when we chaff;
From the quick to the slow it will flicker and flow,
Like the flight of the night into brightness and light:

It's the fast, it's the feast, it's the last anapaest.

MARY HOLTBY

TROCHAIC

Yes – it's Hiawatha's wedding!
Wigwams rise, palatial, poky,
With the peace-pipe's fragrance smoky;
On the leafy pathways treading
Goatskinned squawlets hokey-cokey;
Comes the moment all are dreading –
Licensed jester getting joky:
Tales of japes and songs of bedding,
All authentically folky,
Uttered in quadruple trochee.

MARY HOLTBY

*

PENTAMETER

TROCHAIC

Hooray Henry was a rugger hearty,
Maisie was an intellectual maiden;
He came to escort her to a party,
With a dozen lager cartons laden.

Always she'd been taught that booze was sinful,
Hadn't tasted alcoholic liquors –
All too soon, alas, she'd had a skinful –
And came home a lass without her knickers!

W. F. N. WATSON

ANAPAESTIC

Norman Conquest or She was Only a Tanner's Daughter But She was Easily Suede

Over peasants and piglets, Duke Robert, with bold eyes a-blaze,
Came a-cantering, baleful as bear and more randy than goat:
Fair Arlotta had just washed her smalls 'neath the walls of
 Falaise
And was standing there stripped to the buff for a dip in the
 moat,
Never dreaming Duke Robert would grab her and bonk her;
 or, come
To that, make her in consequence, William the Conqueror's
 Mum.

W. F. N. WATSON

IAMBIC
Theological Collage

The Hindu deity, one oft observes,
Opts for a consort sumptuously blest:
Imprimus with exuberance of curves
Her femininity is roundly stressed;

Item of ox-mild almond eyes, a brace;
One pair full lips, one placid smiling mouth;
One nose, one neck, one comely heart-shaped face,
And opulent profusion further south;

Item one torso, lib'rally equipped,
Whose domed addenda gravitation spurn;
One small waist, parabolically hipped;
Twin ample demi-cantaloupes astern;

Two thighs, graced with superabundant charms,
And last of all, at least three pairs of arms.

W. F. N. WATSON

*

HEXAMETER

Heartache springs from classical rules attempted in English.
Quantity does not speak to us roundly, but only bewilders.
Stress misleads us. A trochee cannot replace any spondee
But that found as sixth foot of each intractable item.
Once the struggle is over, what's left sounds very far from
Verse, although F. L. Lucas had heard that Greeks of today can,
Reading our texts, stress the accented syllables, while they
Still make Homer sound like Homer. There's an enigma.

Metres dependent on stress can seem, after that, like a doddle.
No more elisions need vex us nor yet anxious thoughts of hiatus,
And, what is more, you will find that in each line the crucial caesura
Almost takes care of itself, and the whole thing is really quite easy.
Nevertheless, there lurks one danger which should be avoided
(Not a great danger, though, being so very untempting):
If there occurs in the fifth foot a spondee instead of a dactyl,
Rhythm will suffer; and therefore the spondaic line is a rare one.

M. R. MacINTYRE

*

THE ALEXANDRINE

Six feet, twelve syllables: the Alexandrine's there,
Used in great plays by Racine, Corneille, Molière.
Why, when the French can use the form without a qualm,
Do Alexandrines fill the English with alarm?
I'll introduce a rhyme internally; now see
It's not the same this time: the form appears to be
A sort of ballad jog, trod over and again,
As dull as any dog, unsubtle and a pain.
I take the rhyme away, and still the tramp goes through:
We try for all we're worth to break the line in two.
The French make this sound grand, telling impassioned dreams
In their slow, stately tongue, dwelling on mighty themes;
But Anglo-Saxon stops and starts again in jerks.
Show me one poem where the Alexandrine works.
In Riding Rhyme of course it has a sort of place,
But there in every other line we have a change of pace.
Our classic poets, for the greatest part,
In decasyllables display their art;
Just now and then, as in *The Faerie Queene*,
Care to avoid monotony is seen,
And you will find a stanza's closing line
Become a useful Alexandrine, as does mine.

PAUL GRIFFIN

THE CAESURA

Caesuras are just pauses in a line:
Here comes a rest. Feel better now? Oh, fine!
That line had two Caesuras; this has one
The best fall near the middle. It's quite fun
To let your verse go tidily along,
Decasyllabic in its natural song,
For perfect lines have music of their own;
But never let them sink to monotone;
Give them variety; let them take breath
Before you bore your audience to death.

One piece of advice: the longer your lines are, the poorer
They're bound to appear if you let them go roaming without a Caesura.

PAUL GRIFFIN

*

THE IAMBIC PENTAMETER

A Short History

Part I

Faire *Chaucer* gotte ther ferste: bifor hys tyme
Al was *aliteracioun*, nat ryme.
(The *Anglo-Saxonne* poets cam compleyte
With, metricaly spekynge, two lefte feyte.)
Hys *Caunterbury Tales* in couplets slye
Dissect societie, it is no lie.

Then comes the *Sonet*, indisputed king
Of lyrick verse. Devysed in Italie,
Its prototypick rhyme-scheme's twice *ab*
BA – thus mightie *Petrarch*'s octaves ring –
With sestet of a double *cde*.
Great *Shakespeare* rang the changes on this form:

77

His quatrains run *abab, cd*
cd (thus Anglicizing Petrarch's norm);
The third is neatly capp'd with humorous
Or barbed or antithetick couplet – *thus.*

The plays, with some exception, do eschew
Such well-wrought scheming, for their grander themes
Are better served by verse entirely blank,
That will adapt to each dramatick twist
And not be fetter'd by the tyrant, Rhyme.
(Likewise did *Milton* frame his Epick Song,
In diction ponderously latinate,
Of Disobedience and Godly Ire.)

The next to play on *Iamb*'s tuneful lyre
Were stately *Dryden*, poet laureate,
And nimble *Pope*: perfectors of the great
Heroick couplet, wit's most deadly dart,
Immortalizing *Dulness* in their Art.

The urban (and urbane) Augustan guile
Of waspish satirists at last gave way
To that more rural, meditative style
Which left the world the *Elegy*, by Gray.

Part II

There was a boy – the father to the man
Who in a worthy, wordy *Prelude* wrote
Interminable reminiscences
Of how that boy would hoot at passing owls
And how the owls would echo back those hoots
And suchlike formative experience
Of charming, wholesome, quaintly rural sort.

There was a younger buck of noble stock
Who satirized such stuff in tones sardonic
(Whene'er not posing on some lonely rock
Or crag sublime). His influence cyclonic
Left female readers in a state of nervous shock.
Thus runs his eight-line stanza, called *Byronic*:
Great Byron! Though the Muse swears it's not you she hates,
'Tis true your final couplet oft excruciates.

(Art is immortal, but the winding-sheets
Of death soon covered Byron, and young what-d'ye-call-
Him, Percy Shelley, and consumptive Keats:
Practitioners of odes ornithological.)

And slowly answered noble Tennyson:
Of these above-named poets, Keats is first
In influence; we Late Romantics share
His sensibility. I speak for all.
Sweet *Iamb*'s fluent metre suits us well,
Though skill'd we are enow at *Anapaest*,
Or *Spondee*'s slow, sad march funereal.
No witty rhymes for us, for poesie
Should dwell in distant melancholy halls
And faerie places, far from satire's dart,
In fanciful, archaic diction wrapp'd.

Look! That's my last romantic over there!
Ay – caped he is, with copious, flowing hair
And grizzled beard. Faugh! Such is not for me!
My Muse is metaphysical, you see.
Rhetorical, you ask? – ay, that as well!
Iambic verse? The Browning version's hell
On earth! – it limps along, quite broken-backed,
And somehow is peculiarly packed.
With punctuation. Yet I have – yes! – fans. (A
Conclusion, good as any, for a stanza.)

Sprung rhythm (Hopkins-handled, Anglo-Saxon-
Based) sought to stamp out *Iamb*'s foreign foot.
Thank God! by whose good grace there was no tax on
Alliteration . . .
                        Georgians firmly put
Di-dum di-dum di-dum back on the map,
With diction boring, rhythm even more,
And bloodless sentiment, without a scrap
Of genuine emotion – till the war . . .

It seems that out of English Lit, escaped
These little feet, arranged in fives, that skipped
Through Chaucer, Shakespeare, Milton, Pope and Keats,
Their usefulness outlived. The ghastly sights

Of modern warfare murdered perfect rhyme
And well-wrought rhythm; in the blood-soaked loam
Of Flanders lie their dank, neglected bones.
Though traces can be found in certain lines
By modernists, the great tradition's broken,
And nowadays *vers* liberties are taken
By every common Seamus, Craig or Ted.
Iambics are now well and truly dead.

Envoi

Not quite – for in my humble fashion I've
Attempted here to keep the form alive;
And if it's failed to please, though well-intentioned,
Go back and read the poets that I've mentioned!

PETER NORMAN

*

BLANK VERSE

As Henry Howard, Earl of Surrey, thought,
Blank verse went on, and on, and on, and on;
Each line of it had five iambic feet,
And finished with a punctuation mark.

Marlowe took this, and, with his mighty line,
Startled the angels on the walls of heaven,
Made mountains leap, and oceans stream with blood
To entertain Elizabethan mobs.

Then later writers took blank verse, and made
Their lines run on, as if the fivefold beat
Throbbed like an artery below a skin
Of heightened prose.

        In William Shakespeare's hand
Such methods served the purpose of his art,
With many others, born of mastery:
Short barks of sound, involved magniloquence,

Even looseness, that proved harbinger of a
Terrible decadence and carelessness
Among the inadequate Jacobean writers.

On to the scene, when all seemed dark and void,
Came the blind Milton; as great painters strode
Out of Ferrara, or the Tuscan hills
About Arezzo, to obey the word
Of Quattrocento Popes, and turn their halls
Into a blaze of pageantry; so he,
With mind afire, dictated to his girls
Page after page of epic, such as lives,
Though much neglected, and through Paradise
For ever takes its solitary way.

The limits of the medium explored,
Not Milton's imitators, nor the line
Of High Romantics could do more than show
The graces their great masters had devised.
Yeats gave the form an occasional dance or two,
Fitting in stresses and syllables here and there.

The rest is silence, and John Betjeman.

PAUL GRIFFIN

*

IRREGULARITY

You can use different sorts of feet within one poem, even within a
single line of a poem. It is usually done to create some special effect.

Cargoes

Metre: most distinctive – with successive stanzas
Representing vessels on the open sea,
   With cargoes of punch-words,
   Local colour,
Euphony, and endings going ONE, TWO, THREE.

P. I. FELL

Dead, like an old tea-bag, used and thrown away!
That's what's going to happen to us all some day.
The world's our teapot. How can we get out?
Alas, the only way is up the spout!

GAVIN EWART

*

COMMON MEASURE
(See also 'The Quatrain', page 112)

This is also known as ballad metre, or English hymnal metre; it is the 'eight and six' metre mentioned by Peter Quince in Shakespeare's *A Midsummer Night's Dream*.

O God, our help in ages past,
    Let enterprise be free;
The first be first, the last be last,
    So should it always be.

Our nation has grown too effete,
    The Hand-out State degrades;
Who does not work let him not eat,
    Unless in shares he trades.

The meek, of course, shall have the earth,
    But not till they are dead;
Meanwhile let's raise our songs of mirth
    To capital instead.

O Lord, who healed the sick and thus
    Prolonged their useful days,
The NHS is safe with us
    With more for them as pays.

GERARD BENSON

LONG MEASURE

For those who with uncertain voice
  Wrote hymns and hoped these would survive,
Long Measure was a favourite choice:
  It put them straight in overdrive.
They simply went serenely on
  In octosyllables like this,
With lots of words like 'benison'
  And 'paraclete' and 'hark' and 'bliss'.

No clever rhymes, or thoughtful things
  Unwarranted by psalm or text,
Because, it seems, the King of Kings
  Prefers to know what's coming next.

They'd then await, these blessed bards,
  The heavenly place reserved for them –
For it was always on the cards
  They'd make it to 'Hymns A. & M.'

PAUL GRIFFIN

*

SHORT MEASURE

When you are writing hymns
Here is a pleasant lilt
To match the praise of seraphims
Or carry prayers for guilt.

Short measure is the name
This small device is given,
Though with short measure none can claim
The key to life and heaven.

KATIE MALLETT

*

POULTER'S MEASURE

An oddball form of verse that has uneven lines
Is known as Poulter's measure, which perversely intertwines
Sixes and sevens, giving each couplet mismatched legs.
That generous man, the poulterer, the chap who sold you eggs,
Is he by whom we name it, for – though he was keen –
If you bought two dozen from him he would make the second fourteen.
One scribbler who could use the form quite well was Surrey
But no one bothers now – we moderns always want to hurry,
And lines that limp and stumble and seem somehow wrong
Obstruct us, while heptameters just go on far too long.

TOM AITKEN

TO RHYME OR NOT TO RHYME

On First Looking into a Rhyming Dictionary

How often have I searched for clever rhymes
To ginger up some verse I'd scribbled down,
Ploughed through the *Oxford* with an anxious frown,
Plus *Chambers, Collins, Longmans*; even at times
Considered words from other tongues and climes,
Some *mot juste* – adverb, adjective or noun –
To finish off a limping line, and drown
My creaking measures in melodious chimes.
Then this new dictionary came my way;
Aladdin's Cave! with ever-open door!
Phonetically grouped, in neat array,
Were all the words I had been looking for.
     They tell me rhymes are out of fashion, now.
     Who cares? I'll go on rhyming, anyhow.

STANLEY J. SHARPLESS

*

TYPES OF RHYME

Masculine we call a rhyme
When it makes a single chime.
What is there in manliness
That justifies it? Shall I guess?
It is man who takes a pride
In being quickly satisfied.

A double rhyme, or rhyming trochee
Is feminine. That's not just joky:
It's woman-like, for it's expressing
The double nature she's possessing.
A female's acts are complicated
And never quickly terminated.

No sexist language is distillable
From rhyming on a triple-syllable.
Although in heavenly terms the Trinity
Is used to signify divinity,
On earth two's company, and wearable,
But three's a crowd, and quite unbearable.

PAUL GRIFFIN

*

MONORHYME

MASCULINE ENDINGS

I desire
To retire
To a shire.
I would buy a
Gent's attire
And aspire

To be squire;
Tend my byre
In the mire
(I require
Nothing higher);
Join the choir
For *Messiah*;
Smoke my briar;
And expire
By the fire.

NOEL PETTY

*

FEMININE ENDINGS

Memoranda

So often with dear Alexander
I'd walk amidst the oleander
And down to where the stream's meander
Is flanked with glades of jacaranda,
And there with silken words he fanned a
Flame of such love so pure, so grand. (Ah!
  I little knew he did philander.)
  To every whim with joy I'd pander
  A slave to my supreme commander,
  I the goose, and he the gander.

CATHERINE BENSON

*

TRIPLE RHYME

When writing a poem you want to end cosily
Hoping to make the reader see rosily
Life's thorny path, and travel it easily,
Here is a way to make it go breezily.

With triple rhymes a verse goes on cheerily
No one could say that its metre plods wearily.
Though some might say that it twists the tongue teasingly,
Others will say that it passes quite pleasingly.

KATIE MALLETT

*

DOUBLE END-RHYME

Sid's parties have a Babel-grammar clamour
That more exclusive soirées have not got:
The music hits you like a hammer; glamour
Comes in the shape of Doreen, Charlotte, Dot.

One glass of punch – and watch the ceiling reeling
While Doreen's tango makes the floor see-saw;
Dot's in a clinch and Charlotte's squealing, feeling
As pickled as an onion, but more raw.
Waking next day with stomach churning, burning,
Tongue like a kipper, head like a death-bell knell;
Never again's the message, turning learning
Into experience. It was – well – Hell!

D. A. PRINCE

*

MULTIRHYME

Bad poets who commit the prime rhyme-crime
And use a word that quite prevents dense sense,
Must blench at using this device twice, thrice,
Although a master like our good Hood could.
His rhyming words appear both planned and bland,
In ways that make the most severe ear cheer,
Though the penult should have, I guess, less stress.
His craftsmanship makes many curse worse verse,
And cry with joy at the divine line Nine.
So evermore his skill will thrill, still fill
The soul with mirth, and put to flight night fright.
Tom's Muse, amuse true Sues whose Hughs choose booze!

GAVIN J. S. ROSS

*

INTERNAL RHYME

Do you know, when you eat there are thirty-two feet
  of interior tubing to deal with it?
Allow this to grapple, let's say with an apple –
  it may or may not have the peel with it –
Just imagine the pippin beginning its trip in
  the throat, which adjoins the oesophagus
(It has quitted the mouth on its way to the south,
  like a corpse in a shifting sarcophagus);
And think what befalls as those rubbery walls
  embrace it and knead it between 'em;
What knowledge it learns as it slithers and turns
  and lands up in the dark duodenum. . .
A minimal hummock, it's off to the stomach –
  reduced, so I'm told, by the acid,
Which gives it a spray as it moves on its way,
  and renders it mushy and placid. . .

89

Well, you're getting the picture, but, risking the stricture
   that stories once started should finish,
I propose to omit what is waiting for it
   as its size and its structure diminish.
If I pass unrecorded the subsequent sordid
   adventures that form the diurnal
Dispersion achieved, you should not feel aggrieved –
   I'm confined to the strictly internal.

MARY HOLTBY

Observation

Oh, it may be meretricious, but I find it quite delicious to observe the
  little fishes in the Dee:
But the concrete's old and black and there, inside it (in a crack), I saw a
  tiny stickleback OBSERVING ME.

P. I. FELL

*

LEONINE RHYME

A type of internal rhyme in which the word before the caesura (see page
77) rhymes with the last word of the line.

Lord Tennyson's Revenge

I

On the Isle of Wight one summer's night the Poet Laureate lay
For the news fresh down from London had filled him with dismay:
'Browning wins poetic *fame*! Swinburne greeted with ac*claim*!'
Then sware Lord Alfred *T*.: 'They shall never conquer *me*!
But I've used up every *metre*, and I'm no weak-kneed re*peater*;
I've done verses by the *mile*, using every bardic *style*,
So I'll have to pull some rabbits if I'm still to win the day.

II

'I've done virelais and ballads, I've done lyrics, lays and odes,
I've done every kind of sonnet, I've done every kind of song;
I've done verses on the *Lakes*, I've done cantos and al*caics*,
I've done idylls in cart-*loads*, I've done staves and pali*nodes*;
But I'll have to think of something, for the competition's strong.'

III

Thus he went to bed in *fear*, but awoke with an i*dea*:
'I'll compose an epic poem with some highly varied stressing.
I shall rhyme some in mid-*line*; and call that LEO*NINE*,
And by varying the feet
I shall keep the buggers guessing,
For they'll never fathom what they have to beat.
And at unexpected times
I'll throw in some longer *verses*, so they'll tear their hair with *curses*,
As they try to solve the pattern of the rhymes.'

IV

So he told of England's *glories*, and of Flores in the A*zores*,
And his public rallied round
When they heard the wondrous rattle
Of the new staccato sound.
'See that rhyme at the cae*sura*! His touch has ne'er been *surer*!'
The enemy retreated and was forced to bow the knee
For he'd won the metric battle;
And those upstart would-be *peers* had to wait for fifteen *years*
Till he died the reigning champion at the age of eighty-three.

NOEL PETTY

*

(*Note* Poets nowadays are constrained to have
regard to market forces. Market forces require
cost-cutting. Cost-cutting involves vot using two
or more rhymes where one will suffice.)

Crystal globes that, iridescent
Glowed on trees along the Crescent
In the terraced town of Cheshunt
Where one yet might start (and – yes, end)
Syntheses (of past and present),
Poet shading into peasant . . .
Spring – and mornings luminescent,
Postman calls ('What's Auntie Bess sent
This year? Hardy!'). Effervescent
Soda-syphon. 'How does *Tess* end?'. . .
Winter, with its snow incessant,
Leisured feasts upon roast pheasant:
Limericks by Lear. (Unlessened
Still, one's 'Mr Lear. HOW PLEASANT!')

P. I. FELL

*

Echoes from the Atrium
or
The Praetorian Guard has been Privatized

(*Note* 'Despite scarcity of rhymes in English,
throughout the poem no rhyming syllable should . . .
echo the *full* sound of any other rhyming syllable.
This means that rhymes like . . . "tail/tale", "great/-
grate", "pain/pane", should be avoided' – Swann &
Sidgwick, *The Making of Verse*.)

Wearily Augustus Caesar,
When the hour-glass sands showed '*Six heures*',
Hearing a stentorian 'Tea, sir!',
Set his aide-de-camp the teaser:

'Why, precisely, does this geezer
('Name, *patron*?' 'My name's McGee, sir')
Keep on yelling at me 'Tea, sir!'?
Don't you think his expertise a
Fraction overpriced? ('My fee, sir?')
Ought I to revoke his visa?'

Livia, though – she knows what frees *her*:
'What we *do* need is a freezer!'

P. I. FELL

*

A Homophonically Rhyming Poem

In reverence, I
Approached with awe
Your trifling or
Sarcastic eye.
Belinda, your
Elusive air
Was present e'er
In days of yore.
But say, will you
Remember our
Consummate hour
When laid in yew?

NOEL PETTY

*

EYE RHYMES

The eye rhyme
Is generally used by me
To show how you can rely
On foreign pronunciations to upset the applecart completely.

PAUL GRIFFIN

Euripides
Had grumbling insides:
Sometimes they were like a squadron of planes
And sometimes like the Frogs of Aristophanes.

PAUL GRIFFIN

Dante
Said to a débutante:
'You're not as nice
As Beatrice.'

PAUL GRIFFIN

Max Bruch
Didn't splutter much;
But with Dvořák
You needed an anorak.

PAUL GRIFFIN

*

RIME RICHE

When I am rich I mean to found
A dogs' home for the Lost and Found;
To claim your dog will cost a pound,
And they'll run free, within their pound,
(Except Rottweilers, whose teeth are ground,
And Dobermanns hang above the ground,
And Chows are chained, and Boxers bound.)
When their owners come, how they'll bound
To the great high fence, well-made and sound.
They'll leave there with the loveliest sound
Of grateful barks; they will bark a round:
Woof, yap, woof, yap will echo around.

REM BEL

PARARHYME

The Pararhyme's a sort of halfway house
Between full rhyme and none at all. Its use
Can disconcert: for what the ear expects –
The rounded rhyme the previous line predicts –
Is never heard; instead, a kind of muffled
Echo. Our sense of symmetry is baffled,
Yet satisfied; a mood of vague disturbance
Is conjured up – a *frisson* of discordance.
Such subtlety is most effective where the
Whole atmosphere's intended to be eerie.
In English verse the *locus classicus*
Is Wilfred Owen's poem where, the animus
Of war at last transcended, warriors,
No longer now opposed, throw down the barriers
Of sterile hate and make their spectral meeting,
Through supernatural love, a mystic mating.

MARTIN FAGG

*

ASSONANCE

True assonance in poetry will seldom make it flow,
　　For it's far too much like rhyming that has failed to score a hit:
The vowels you aim to echo, but the consonants you don't,
　　And the ultimate result is to make it sound like this.

In another sort of assonance you mostly change the vowels,
　　Leaving consonants to echo like a carillon of bells,
Rolling off delightfully through valleys and through vales
　　And curling round the consciousness like boomerangs or bowls.

Yet assonance, sweet assonance, is very much like dissonance,
　　Precocious and preposterous, and missing every time:
Its anarchistic pistons seem to lose the joy of unisons
　　And tangle up your thinking, till you seek relief in rhyme.

PAUL GRIFFIN

CONSONANCE

Hack not the oak, butcher not beech nor birch,
Choose not the chestnut to chastise with sticks;
Stuck be its stock, which loves to live in leaves,
Till winds deal wounds and pitch them from their perch.
Then squirrel packs his perks, and boyhood picks:
Trove well contrived for quarrel he retrieves.

MARY HOLTBY

*

BROKEN RHYME

The backstage girls are silent, apprehens-
ively half-nudging one another, bash-
fully, perhaps, more likely miming passionate performances with grim and sense-
less energy. They do not lack bravad-
o, nor that talent bred in them to tit-
ivate the jaded and the parasit-
ical, as those who wait on them with hard-
ened arteries. Now straining, every swoll-
en muscle tugs and tussles while the tass-
els twitch and flinch to tape-recorded cas-
tanets: these stir the soulless and the ol-
eaginous into arthritic ferv-
our, as the nerveless bodies curve and swerve.

BILL GREENWELL

Wanting a poem where each single line must finish with a brok-
en word is totally provoking, calling as it does for ingenuity and curious ming-

ling of poetry and colloqui-
ialisms. I am not jok-
ing. I'll fuel my Muse with sting-
o. Purple bats and blue flaming-
oes whirl around my friendly local as I give the wench a soak-
ing, then, refreshed, pull out my fing-
er. Oh, to Hell with Gavin Ewart! These few lines will have to do.

JOHN STANLEY SWEETMAN

*

GROTESQUE RHYME

When writing for yourself or under someone's aegis
Finding a special rhyme to fit can be extremely tegius.
But if like Ogden Nash you've the verve and gall to do it
Here's a way to pair up rhymes like pieces of a cruet.
So if you find you're stuck, here's a way to solve your problem:
Just twist a word, or think of two and together neatly cobble 'em.
Then everyone will think your work is literarily lustrous
And praise your verse, though most of the time you're simply being
    prepustrous.

KATIE MALLETT

Ogden Nash Poem

The usual verse form adopted by Ogden Nash
Is so flexible that innumerable parodists are tempted to have a bash.
You do not have to reserve excessive time for it;
You simply note the last stressed syllable in the first line of each couplet
    and then carry on the second line until you happen to hit on a
    rhyme for it.
It is really a sort of endless clerihew

97

That leaves you wondering whether the next line is going to end with
   some saying of Nikita Khrushchev, or a reference to the jovial
   Saint of Lincoln, England, or with some truly awful expression
   that only works as a rhyme in Lincoln, Nebraska, or in London,
   Onterihew.
Such verbal haberdashery
Is the true essence of Ogden Nashery.

GAVIN J. S. ROSS

Who Says You Can't Rhyme 'Orange'?

When challenged to rhyme 'Orange',
Scotsman Angus Warren J-
amieson (who sports a kilt and sporran) g-
enially observed: 'Citrus fruits are foreign: J-
affas, for example, come from Israel. One old florin j-
ust about would buy a bagful . . . Who says you can't rhyme
   "Orange"?'!

RON RUBIN

*

SYNTHETIC RHYME

Spelling in English defies cogent thought
As poets and scholars and such can repought,
As idiosyncracies pile up to thwought
Their efforts, no matter how well they've been tought.

Some poets make capital out of this trait
By spelling their rhymes in the logical wait,
Which makes them look comic, though possibly thait
(The poets) have used them whilst being risquait.

KATIE MALLETT

*

PRUNED RHYME

Pruned Poem

The poem (pruned) is though, I *grant*;
It makes the poet curse and *rant*,
'Though labouring like th' proverbial *ant*.

He must all lofty form *eschew*
And at a set of letter*s chew*
To mould the sense and metre *hew*.

And so each final word's *estate*
Is left in a truncated *state*
Like many artists in the *Tate*.

Note from the front the words *erode*
As though his Muse a cart-horse *rode*
(Not Pegasus) to make this *ode*.

Pruned poems, howsoe'er they *start*
End up as something of a *tart*,
And suffer for the sake of *art*.

D. A. PRINCE

Overheard in a Market-place Pub

Forgive me if this all sounds *stale*,
But please, sir, listen to my *tale*.
(Oh, thanks, I'll have a pint of *ale*.)

In years gone by when just a *sprig*,
And, thinking back, a little *prig*,
I ventured out in my best *rig*.

I couldn't wait to make a *start*.
And then I met this smashing *tart*.
Oh yes, I knew the caveman's *art*.

Said I, when turning on the *charm*,
'Come on, my poppet, where's the *harm*?'
I really meant to chance my *arm*.

Dead certain of my macho *skill*,
I closed right in to make the *kill*.
The time was ripe – for good or *ill*.

But then I got a stinging *clout*.
This charming creature called me '*lout*'.
She seemed a tiny bit put *out*.

She smacked my hands and said 'You *brat*!
Go back to school, you little *rat*!
What do you think you're playing *at*?'

I crept back to my market *stall*.
I felt that I was two feet *tall*.
I'd learned a lot. I think that's *all*.

FRANK RICHARDS

*

FIRST-WORD RHYME

What fiend has set us such a fearful task –
To write a poem where the rhymes occur,
Not at the end but at the line's beginning?
Do you suppose it's possible at all?

All right! Let's make a start but, first, we'll curse
His ancestors and all his kith and kin;
Call down the wrath of heaven upon him too.
This done we shall proceed in proper form.

So we must choose a theme. Let it be such
That fertile fancy may full freely roam;
No limits should be set to genius' play;
At least no more than there already are.

But there's one limit that we must observe;
It's laid down in the rules. Just sixteen lines
Cut off imagination's furious flow;
Wits curdled, we can end the matter here.

JOHN STANLEY SWEETMAN

BACK-TRACK RHYMING

Loves and Hates

Love your gear, but
Hate your beer gut.

GAVIN EWART

*

RHYMED VERSE DISGUISED AS PROSE

To help us on life's busy road, a road both steep and long, a draught so fine that will revive is cordial Patience Strong. Too long has she rejected been, too long bethought as square; now of her splendid poesy have we become aware. For we've refound her noble verse, relearnt her wisdom fine, her genteel way of saving space, and her language, rich as wine. Her verses show life's weft and woof, both in sunshine and in showers; the sparkling dew upon the grass, the birds and bees and flowers. Oh, let us now praise Penguin Books, who offer us this crown, this diadem of priceless pearls, as light as thistledown. So let's in triumph glasses raise and hymn in happy song the poets of great England's prime: Will Shakespeare and Miss Strong.

E. O. PARROTT

*

SKELTONIC OR TUMBLING VERSE

Named after John Skelton, a Tudor poet whose detractors referred to his works as 'rude rayling', this verse form uses short lines and is full of devices such as multiple rhyme, alliteration, etc.

There are bits in Skeltonics
That shine like an onyx,
But mostly they run
Without being much fun
On a course that at times
Seems driven by rhymes.
Their tone is thrasonical,
Seldom euphonical,
Hoarse and ironical,
Like an early McGonagall.
John Skelton had venom; he
Made many an enemy
By boring like a weevil
In a time of upheaval
When Henry the Eight
Was putting things straight.
Skelton's ambition
Had not much tradition
To help in his mission,
Which was part satirical,
Part panegyrical,
But sometimes a miracle
When bright colour shines
Out of crude lines
Like a blossom grown
In a heap of stone;
And you think: 'Why not I?
I'll give it a try.'

PAUL GRIFFIN

Overheard in a City Bar

You're barred,
You tub of lard.
Get out,
You lout!
Just sup
That up,
And go!
Just blow!
You're stinking drunk,
You blazered hunk,
You clothed gorilla,
You lager-swiller.
I'm telling you,
I've better things to do
Than serving well-dressed apes,
You jackanapes.
So just piss off,
You imitation toff,
You half-trained puppy,
You yuppy,
Just hit the track,
And don't come back;
And take your Gucchi shoes
And cave-man views,
You turd-brained bore,
To someone who'll appreciate them more.
Don't answer back,
You natterjack,
You dipsomaniac,
Yack, yack, yack, yack.
Just button up, you prat.
Don't speak to me like that.
You've got a bloody nerve.
You needn't think I'll serve
You,
Or your bloody crew
Gin and champagne
Ever again.

You teenage bankers
Are all a load of wankers.
So
Go!
And don't come back tomorrow.

(Parting is such sweet sorrow.)

GERARD BENSON

*

FREE VERSE

Verse,
Free of all rules
Of rhythm and rhyme.

First refuge of those
Who cannot tell
An iambic pentameter
From
A Pickfords pantechnicon.

Its anarchical formlessness
Enables lazy lovers
To pour their emotions on the page,
Line by uneven line,
And call it
Poetry.

Their collected works,
Duly xeroxed and stapled,
Take longer to read
Than they took to write.

Still, it's a free country –
Isn't it?
Poetic freedom-fighters unite.
Let my poem go!

V. E. COX

Free verse
Is really
and sadly *un*ideally
written-for-a-fee verse.
Free is 'only what it's *called*'
(a phrase that's been forestalled
by the White Knight).
Poets expect quite
20p a line,
and they
would say
that's cutting it
a bit
fine.
But if you ask me,
that'd be
okey-doke
for the stony-broke;
and the mercenary
literary
or crafty-arty
literati
would then
take pen
and write tomes
of long thin pomes
(like this
one is)
so that a
fatter
purse
would reward their verse.
But if wider and shorter verses were to be preferred,
You can bet they'd flog them at so much a word.

JOYCE JOHNSON

*

What mocking fiend invented the ballade?
    It must have had its origins in Hell.
The Snake who caught deluded Eve off guard
    (After his earlier efforts to rebel)
Had leisure to consider, when she fell,
    With what he next might occupy his time . . .
So Cain cried out, when Abel wrote too well,
    'I'd give my soul to find another rhyme!'

Of course the Devil's followers are tarred
    With the same brush – their aims are parallel –
Procrustes, the ingenious de Sade,
    And Grand Inquisitor, eager to quell
A heretic, could make their victims yell.
    So we who serve the Muse commit no crime,
Yet to what agony her whips compel!
    I'd give my soul to find another rhyme.

By now you've realized the task is hard:
    Poetry asks an inch but takes an ell;
And, once embarked, behold the helpless bard
    Cursing his useless craft, the cockleshell
In which he thought to ride above the swell;
    Not toss in raging storms or sink in slime,
Crying, 'O save me! I'm prepared to sell –
    I'd give my soul to find another rhyme!'

Envoi

Tyro, avoid this fate, content to dwell
    On less demanding forms; you see that I'm
So anxious to complete the tale I tell
    I'd give my soul to find another rhyme.

MARY HOLTBY

*

A Monorhyme Protest

A lot of modern verse is free,
And of course it ought to be;
In fact I often think that *we*
Should charge the poet a reading fee.

PHILIP A. NICHOLSON

*

The Modern Poet

Loitering in seedy pubs, praying some Muse
Will slouch in, Soho-pale, just fit to use
Ideas sharp-suited admen haven't found
For Cola look-alikes and CD sound,
Poets – once aristo, or Welsh, or drunk –
Still sidle slyly out, or do a bunk,
As ever leaving bills unpaid, their verse unread,
And lives as sordid as an unmade bed,
Like Chatterton's, whose exploits fictionary
Were cobbled from some rhyming dictionary.
The British like their poets red, but dead,
Like Morris, MacNeice, Auden – enough said –
Despite their lurking passion for aesthetes
And verbal puzzles: d'you say Yeats or Yeats?
But living poets, hard-edged, taut, uneasy,
Turn bourgeois consciences a trifle queasy.

D. A. PRINCE

*

STANZAS AND SUCHLIKE

THE COUPLET

This is probably the commonest 'unit' of rhymed poetry and verse. It is much used by Shakespeare, especially in his early plays, and even more by the writers of pantomime. Elsewhere in this volume it appears in such diverse forms as the clerihew, the ruthless rhyme and the limerick. A grotesque form of the couplet is the basis of the verse of Ogden Nash.

CHAUCERIAN COUPLETS

A Rhymester was there in the company,
Who wrought with Parrott in that industry
Of writing books that would all folk advise
How they might, though unlearned, seem full wise
And pass at once for scholars. This essay
Had not enriched him and he went alway
In casual vesture with an untrimmed beard,
And was, in sooth, in aspect something weird.

He was, in years, a little past the prime,
Yet was he skilled in prosody and rhyme.
He could make limericks and clerihews
On any person famous in the News,
And turn a sonnet or a triolet
In half an hour, his whistle being wet.
Of strophe and antistrophe he was a master,
He was indeed a perfect Poetaster.

JOHN STANLEY SWEETMAN

The Prelude
(After William Wordsworth)

In many a scenic and populous spot,
He was seeing the sights. And was THINKING A LOT.

P. I. FELL

HEROIC COUPLETS

A form with very tight parameters,
Heroic Couplets use pentameters.
Their mood can vary – sad or dithyrambic;
Their metre, though, must always be iambic.
The purists (and the pedants) have ordained
Each couplet must be strictly self-contained:
The sentiment the starting line began
Completed in its all-too-narrow span.
But those who find this edict far too taxing
Adopt a mode that's rather more relaxing;
And let (as I am doing now) their text
Spill over from one couplet to the next.
Such lofty eloquence must, clearly, rhyme,
Resounding with richly ringing chime
(Though most permit such verse at times to wear
A rhyme that greets the eye but not the ear).
The thought must be transparent – never muddied;
The tone – precise, astringent, brisk yet studied.

Heroic Couplets – does the pompous name
Imply that verse so-called must always frame
The macho feats of marble-muscled heroes,
Ignoring peasants, pedlars, pirates, pierrots
And all such lowly persons? Not at all.
To demonstrate the opposite, recall
The *oeuvre* of maestro Alexander Pope,
A bard whose magical technique could cope
So well with their demands, his couplets seem
As silken as the surface of a stream.
His great cod-epic makes a huge affair
Revolve around the ravishing of hair
From poor Belinda's bonce – a mighty *coup*!
Thus, couplets can be *mock*-heroic too,
Exposing, by deft metrical invention,
The gap between Man's worth and his pretension.

MARTIN FAGG

*

TRIPLETS AND TERCETS

If you add a rhyming line to a couplet you get (surprise, surprise) a triplet. In *terza rima* (see page 111) where the rhymes of the three-line stanzas intertwine, these stanzas are known as tercets. In the Petrarchan, or Italian, sonnet (see page 165), the final sestet consists of two tercets.

TENNYSONIAN TRIPLETS

When Tennyson was sore bereaved
He wrote a poem as he grieved
In form like clover – triple-leaved.

The verse is short, the rhyme the same
To carry gloom, despair or blame,
A simple but sufficient frame.

Though Tennyson went on and on
Until his morbid Muse had gone,
It need not be a marathon.

But when describing death or art,
Or just lamenting from the heart,
Concluding is the hardest part.

KATIE MALLETT

TERCETS AND TERZA RIMA

We English poets seldom rhyme in threes,
And, when we do, choose simple rhymes like these;
Italian poets rhyme with greater ease,

Because their language skips like a Bacchante:
It's full of rhymes, while English rhymes are scanty,
A fact which makes it hard to translate Dante.

When he began the Comedy Divine
He wrote, not triplets, as I have above,
But *terza rima*, where the lines entwine,

The trios fit together like a glove
While a fresh rhyme arriving on the scene
Offers the older rhymes a farewell shove

By forcing a new presence in between:
Until in turn it has to say 'bung-ho!' –
Another rhyme beginning the beguine;

And so through Hell and Purgatorio
Out of the foul Satanic atmosphere
The Master trips it with unerring toe

To Paradise (where Beatrice's near)
As if to say to any rival poet:
'Abandon hope all ye who enter here.'

I couldn't keep it up so long, I know it:
This *terza rima* has me pale and quaking;
After one canto I'd be bound to blow it,

And lose the thread of all my undertaking.

PAUL GRIFFIN

111

'It's Spring,' I said, and paused with ardent meaning,
'The season of true-lovers'-knots' renewing.'
Said she: 'I'll have to think about spring cleaning.'

'It's Spring,' I pleaded, still intent on wooing;
'The birds and bees have long since started mating.'
She mused: 'The front-room carpet needs shampooing.'

'It's Spring!' I sighed; 'You're just not concentrating;
Time for Romance – don't pour cold water on it.'
She said: 'The bathroom needs redecorating.'

'It's Spring,' I breathed; 'For you I'd write a sonnet –'
The path of dalliance doggedly still treading.
She murmured: 'Now what bee is in your bonnet?'

'Oh well,' I mumbled, 'I've Spring plants for bedding,'
All hope abandoning as mere delusion.
'Bedding?' she cried, preoccupation shedding,

And brought the matter to its due conclusion.

W. F. N. WATSON

*

THE QUATRAIN

This is one of the most commonly used stanza forms in all poetry and may be rhymed or unrhymed. The ballad stanza, also known as common measure or the English hymnal stanza, is a quatrain, as is Omar Khayyam's *rubai* (see page 118).

Verse for All Seasons

In the Spring a young man's fancy
Lightly turns to poetry,
Writing odes to Rose or Nancy
Corseted in symmetry.

In the dog days of high Summer
He'll compose a doleful song,
Happy to become a strummer
On his guitar, all day long.

In the Autumn, like a bonfire
Fanned to life again, he flames
In his verses with desire
For girls he's seen that have no names.

In the Winter, warmly shuttered,
He extols pure wedded bliss;
As the candle's slowly guttered,
Trades his quatrains for a kiss.

MARGARET ROGERS

*

The Peking Palace

The Peking Palace sits athwart the height –
A stately structure; on the road thereto
A horde of suppliants hurry through the night,
Eager to swell the ever-lengthening queue.

Beyond the Golden Entrance, light and shade
Mingle to summon up mysterious shapes –
Rich artefacts of amber and of jade,
And (limned on silk-stuffs) dragons, cats and apes.

Wrought by Circassian flutes and Tartar bells,
Soft melodies from deep recesses sound;
A hundred subtle Oriental smells
Throughout the spacious premises abound.

A functionary stands within the Hall,
Who knows but little of my barbarous tongue.
No matter! High above, a massive scrawl
Covered in symbols from the roof is hung.

I progress, tortoise-like, along the line;
At last, at long, long last I head the queue.
The functionary's questing eyes meet mine –
In Mandarin Chinese, he calls out, 'Yu!'

I point up to the scrawl: 'A twenty-four,
An eighty-three,' I cry. 'Make that one twice.'
Then, as an afterthought, I speak once more,
'With all, a double portion of fried rice!'

T. L. McCARTHY

A Ballad

'I have the wind today, my lass,
    But thank you for that salad;
It's you must do the washing up,
    For I'm going to write a ballad.'

He hadna writ a line or twa,
    A line but barely three –
Oh, this is how they tell you things
    In the world of balladry –

He hadna writ a line or twa,
    A line but barely trey,
When he scratched his heid, and cried out loud:
    'Why do I talk this way?

'Why do I break into Scottish brogue
    When Scots is what I'm not?
And if I'm going to write some more
    Shouldn't I have a plot?

'The reason I break into Scottish brogue
    And sail this perilous sea
Is the helpful rhymes; as anyone kens
    Wha gleeks wi' half an ee.

'And if I want a plot that's good,
    I must choose from characters three:
The Devil himself, and Robin Hood,
    And the Queen of Faerie.'

He's laid his pen upon his lip,
    And he's looking quite perplexed;
Oh, that's because he doesna ken
    What on earth comes next.

II

He's laid his pen upon his lip
    Till he draws the bitter bluid,
For thinking on the Faerie Queen,
    And Clootie, and Robin Hood.

But he canna see what part they play
    In the song he sings sae fine;
And tick! tock! it's four o'clock,
    And he's written stanzas nine.

'I've written stanzas nine, my lass,
    And it's time for a wee bit break;
So I won't say no to a warming cup
    And a slice or twa of cake.

'I have the wind today, my lass,
    And it looks like a dirty night,
So lay your arm across my breast
    And *tell me what to write!*'

PAUL GRIFFIN

The Mutiny on the Alibi

It was the MY *Alibi*,
Owned by Gawayn de Berri,
And he had oared Miss Jones aboard
As was his secretary.

He made a pile and lived in style,
A TV-film producer,
Who on his boat took her afloat
Intending to seduce her.

They left the Lee-on-Solent quay
Till land was just a speck;
Miss J in her bikini lay
Sun-bathing on the deck.

Now, she had thought that he had brought
Of other guests a squad,
But once offshore she found no more
Than they two on their tod.

Then he intones: 'Yo-ho! Miss Jones,
For your twin hulls I've hankered;
So would you sigh a fond 'Aye! Aye!'
If I to you gets anchored?'

But she cries: 'NAY! No easy lay
Am I; stop! That's enough!'
'Heave-to!' he rants. 'Off with them pants!'
And starts to play it rough.

But what this so-and-so don't know
Is that her Dad (or Pater)
Served twenty trips in HM ships
As Wireless Operator,

And his dear child has learnt and filed
From this wise old ex-tar
Signals Procedures, and, indeed,
To Know What Sailors Are.

So when this prize sea-serpent tries
Her First/Mate for to be,
His grip she slips and quickly nips
To switch on the R/T.

From Harry Rock to Portsmouth Dock,
From Lyme to Plymouth Hoe,
They heard him press her to say yes,
They heard her answer: 'NO!'

116

They heard him say: 'I'll have me way!'
Heard her reply: 'You're plastered!
Take your crude clutch from off me crutch,
You lecherous old bastard!'

He chased her next all round the decks
But in one moment tiny,
Hard by the stern, with one quick turn,
She tips him in the briny.

Then back she goes on twinkling toes –
Oh buoy! Her step was springy –
The wheel to get, and R/T set,
While he crawls in the dinghy.

'MAYDAY!' she signalled, 'SOS',
In Clear and Morse; what's more,
Made signal flags from his white bags
And sent in Semaphore.

From Hastings, Hove and Lulworth Cove,
From Weymouth and Torbay,
Came scores of craft both fore and aft,
To help her on her way.

And as they led her up Spithead
Loud sirens blared in turn,
To see her go with him in tow
Inglorious astern.

At Lee her ears rang with their cheers
And rattling of tin balers,
But raspberries blast as he goes past,
Blown rudely on loud-hailers.

The *Yachting Mail* headlined the tale,
And in all quayside pubs
His name is *merde*; he's never dared
Join any sailing clubs.

So yachtsmen true from Leith to Looe,
Heed this disastrous ode:
Don't force an amatory course
On girls as know Morse Code.

W. F. N. WATSON

Rubá'iyát

(According to Edward Fitzgerald)

When first I set my trembling Hand to write
The *rubá'iyát*, I found it was a Fight
   To rhyme four Times upon a single Sound;
It used to cost me Hours of Sleep at Night.

Old Omar Khayyam, writing Persian Verse
Encountered different Problems, maybe worse;
   Reading between his Lines, one cannot help
But see he must have stifled many a Curse.

But putting Nouns in Capitals, you know,
And dropping Persian Names like Billy-ho –
   Names like Mushtari, Jamshyd and Mahmud –
I learnt to write my Verse Fortissimo.

Life was a Caravan upon its Way,
And Youth all Love and Flowers and Wine, I'd say,
   To hide the Fact that in the general Fuss
One of my Rhymes had gone on Holiday.

Ah, Reader, should you pause from drinking Wine
And spot the Rhyme that's lost from my Design,
   Refill your Glass and smile; what Use to mourn
The Imperfection of your Life, and mine?

PAUL GRIFFIN

Alcaics

Terrible Alcaics! how can I write you,
Sitting in a rain storm, wringing out wet socks?
   Could there be a grimmer setting?
     That is no place to compose Alcaics.

Nobody who's sensible writes them in English;
Hard as he tries to, calamity will follow;
   Horace, living in sunny Italy
     Had quite a different scene to work in.

If I only lived there, bathed in the sunshine,
Dry would my socks be, golden my verses;
  Neither English words nor weather
    Seem to be right for the Alcaic stanza.

PAUL GRIFFIN

*

THE QUINTAIN

In 'Kubla Khan' did Coleridge
A Quintain verse devise,
And in that other 'Rime' of his
It pops up now and then. It is
A tilting-post likewise.

JOYCE JOHNSON

*

THE SESTET

Any six-line stanza, or the second part of a sonnet. Famous practitioners: Burns and Shakespeare.

THE BURNS STANZA

For ilka Scot wha pens a ditty
And seeks tae moralize a bittie
There is a stanza (more's the pity!)
    Wha gaes like this.
Sin' only Burns could make it witty,
    They ca'ed it his.

The Burns or Scottish stanza's sure
Tae find a place in literature;
Like haggis tae the epicure
      It's truly Scots:
It reeks o' mountain, loch, and moor
      Tae patriots.

Och, Sassenachs will ca' it cliquey
An' say its best-laid schemes are creaky;
Let them be generous, no' cheeky:
      It will suffice
For praisin' kilts an' cockaleekie
      An' hailin' mice.

PAUL GRIFFIN

A Lost Poem by R. Burns

I may ha' rags about my bum
And locks as dirty as the lum,
A belly big as ony drum,
      But I'm a bard.
And where I go the lasses come;
      My cock is hard.

Frae Berwick up to John O'Groats
I had my way and sowed my oats
Like ane of Clooty's towzie goats
      I fathered bairns,
Took down my breeks as well as notes
      On braes and cairns.

FIONA PITT-KETHLEY

THE VENUS AND ADONIS STANZA

Adonis, mortal, had the nerve to play
It cool in lovely Venus's embrace.
When asked to make a date, he'd only say
'Tomorrow? No – tomorrow is the Chase.'
(This stanza form we're using, by the way,
Is known as, very briefly, V. and A.)

And chase it was. But who, pray, was the prey?
Adonis fled the Goddess, it is true,
But fell by fatal tusk of boar at bay.
And thus our tale is told in only two
Iambic stanzas. Who needs any more?
Shakespeare, of course, took over ninety-four.

JOYCE JOHNSON

Venus and Adonis in the Underworld – A Fragment

'Okay then, Loverboy,' she says, 'since I
'Ave gotcher darbied in this armlock's span,
I'll be your heist, an' you my villain; try
To do me like I was a wages van;
Snatch from me kisser first; with that as base,
Work south, Luv, where there's other joints to case;

'For on my patch there's jobs enough I trust;
A berkeley's vault you'll find is up for grabs;
Prime stick-ups too, me private pads, to bust,
Where it's quite safe for you to leave your dabs.
Then be my front-man in Love's break-in larks,
The Fuzz shan't cop you, though 'arf London narks.'

Now right turned on, she ennarf in a state,
Like 'e's a fuse an' she a charge of gelly;
But wot a flamin' let-down for 'er, Mate,

For will 'e see 'er right? Not on yer nelly.
It turns out 'e's a jack, from Scotland Yard,
So in a flash, she puts the boot in – 'ard!

W. F. N. WATSON

*

THE SEPTET

RHYME ROYAL

Rhyme royal's really very entertaining:
Its seven-line stanzas tell a tidy tale.
Pentameters (iambic) beat explaining
Your plot in limping ballad forms that fail.
Although at triple rhymes some poets quail,
Remember Shakespeare faced it, undismayed,
And Chaucer, writing *Troilus and Criseyde*.

The twentieth century finds it still alive
And kicking dustiest forms out of the door;
Forms 'large enough to swim in' will survive:
It suits light verse, ingenious rhymes – and, more,
Wit's quite at home within its formal law.
The best's a rambling letter sent by Auden
From Iceland straight to Byron (Lord George Gordon).

The cosy final couplet tucks it in
And offers ample scope for *outré* learning:
This good-night kiss, this cracker-motto's twin
Still suits the well-read browser who's discerning
And thinks a poet's much too good for burning.
To sum up: whether factual or fictive
Rhyme royal is a form that's quite addictive.

D. A. PRINCE

I wolde to Godde that I the purs had bene
    Of ony othere wyght but ye, Chaucere!
Your pleynt upon my emtynesse I ween
    To be falsfounded and of hevy chere.
      Who wroghte my droghte but ye, my rhymestere?
Untill thatte tyme ye get mor than ye spende
I languysshe shal for daies withouten ende.

'Beth hevy ageyn!' ye seye; what can ye mene?
    Untill ye fil me, I moghte dangle here
Lyk to a geldynges bagge, both lyght and lene;
    If that a merchauntes tresorie I were
      I wold ful bulgie and ful fatte appere.
Sith I am youres, my povre poete frend,
I languysshe shal for daies withouten end.

GERARD BENSON

*

THE OCTET

Any eight-line stanza, or the first part of a sonnet.

OTTAVA RIMA

You want a verse form? Try the sunny clime
Of Italy, where poets always thrive.
Is it the grape? Whatever prompts their rhyme
And keeps the art of poetry alive
The fourteenth century proved a lively time
For patenting a stanza to survive.
So Byron put his well-known sexual schemer
Into Boccaccio's style, *ottava rima*.

123

Don Juan fits his eight-line stanzas well:
They give him scope to play the mock-heroic.
Almost burlesque, and, still this side of Hell,
He needn't try to imitate the Stoic
By choosing dreary lodging-rooms to dwell
Or pond'ring learned matters Palaeozoic.
And so each stanza-trimming couplet finds our wencher
Leaping crutch-deep in amorous adventure.

D. A. PRINCE

THE SICILIAN OCTAVE
(Rhyme-scheme *ab*, and that's that)

When Echo echoes only once,
   That's natural. But when a third
Repeat ensues . . . ! (Perhaps the sun's
   The cause of something so absurd?)
In Syracuse they're used to *tons*
   Of encores, and a singing bird
Receives prolonged applause for runs
   Of music they've already heard.

P. I. FELL

*

THE NINE-LINE STANZA

Spenser his long, long tale of Faerie drew out
   Using this stanza, which he had invented,
And here broad hints of allegory threw out
   As Una's dire misfortunes he lamented
And Deadly Sins in grim parade presented:

All in a rather fancy rhyme-scheme, tacked
On five-fold footage, evenly accented,
    Till the ninth line, which, curiously, he packed
With extra syllables – to run like this, in fact.

MARY HOLTBY

Like those machines which labour, turn on turn,
    In some vast packing plant, while silent stare
Their grave attendants on the goods they churn,
    Spenserian Stanzas roll and rumble there,
    Doing their job, though it is hard to bear
The sight of such impersonal machines
    Packing wild thoughts, which are their constant fare,
Into tame stanzas as one packs sardines,
As neat and unemphatic as a row of beans.

PAUL GRIFFIN

*

MATTERS OF FORM

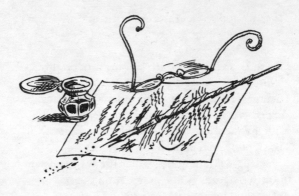

THE BALLADE FAMILY

The most popular form of the ballade, much loved by Belloc, Chesterton and their contemporaries, consists of three eight-line stanzas, rhymed on three rhymes, with a four-line envoi that matches the rhyming scheme of the second half of the stanzas. The last line of all the stanzas, and that of the envoi, are identical, forming the refrain. The prince frequently addressed in the envoi is thought to represent the Prince of Darkness.

Variations on the ballade include those with five stanzas, those with ten-line verses, and the chant royal, which is a very early form. Examples of all these follow.

A Boring Ballade

I'm required to compose a ballade, so let's see:	*a*
I wonder what structure and style I should use?	*b*
The standard form, yes that's most likely to be	*a*
(For a clueless beginner) the right one to choose,	*b*

Though of course in the end it depends on the Muse.   *b*
    It's bound to be tricky for sir has decreed   *c*
That examples like this must instruct *and* amuse –   *b*
    Who wants a ballade that is boring to read?   *c*

Fourteen B-rhymes, that's a lot you'll agree –
    Forgive the self doubt but I'm deep in the blues;
To get through this lot I may yet have to flee
    To the fragile support of tobacco and booze.
Why did I begin, who would be in my shoes,
    What devilish pact have I signed and agreed,
How can I cope without blowing a fuse,
    Who wants a ballade that is boring to read?

Well, I've reached the last verse, and clearly I see
    That so far my efforts can only bemuse;
No matter, ten lines and then I'll be free –
    Next time I'm approached I'll damn well refuse;
It's not worth the hassle whatever ensues.
    Ballades of the past emanate from a breed
Of poets with the talent to stir and enthuse;
    Who wants a ballade that is boring to read?

Envoi

That's it! from a tuckered-out pen-pusher who's
    Watching his faint hope of glory recede;
Don't bother to phone me, I'm off on a cruise –
    Who wants a ballade that is boring to read?

PHILIP A. NICHOLSON

A Ballade of Undue Prolixity

Whereas, last Tuesday, when the midday sun
Had painted arabesques across the bay,
And I consumed a second currant bun
While hankering for underdone *filet*
(Though not neglecting to improve the day
Devising ways of winning at Mah-Jong),
I heard myself emit a sigh and say:
'This sentence is inordinately long!'

I let my mind in retrospection run
Across the decades, to a school at Bray
Where I, the task of 'composition' done,
Against my expectation of an 'A',
Got 'C', and Mr Aloysius Fay
Explained precisely where I had gone wrong:
'Have you not heard of punctuation, pray?
This sentence is inordinately long.'

What webs of consequence those words have spun –
What depths of perturbation they betray!
The men who do the pools and like a pun
Go glassy-eyed and say they cannot stay;
I sense the distant sound of an affray,
I hear the headlines clamour, like a gong –
As: 'Literary man has feet of clay:
This sentence is inordinately long!'

Envoi

Prince, do not turn the key and go away;
Those ancient mortices are very strong!
(Remission for good conduct maybe, eh?
This sentence is inordinately long.)

P. I. FELL

A Ballade of Convenient Refreshment

I must pay tribute to that noble lord
Who would not leave his gambling just to eat,
Whereat the harassed cooks and scullions roared:
'We cannot send him a mere hunk of meat!'
'Wrap it in bread made from the finest wheat!'
A keen inventive chef was heard to call;
The Earl, thereafter, oft-times would repeat:
'I think I'll have a sandwich after all!'

Give me some honest grub I can afford!
Even the *table d'hôte* has got me beat;
The *à la carte*, of course, should be ignored;
I find this gourmet chat much too effete!

128

Let's have food simple, nourishing yet neat.
Summon the waiter, that obsequious Gaul:
'I will not take the *Poulet Marguerite*!
I think I'll have a sandwich after all!'

I do not like a groaning festive board.
I will not join the dining club élite.
I hate those places where champagne is poured,
And fawning minions bow me to my seat.
I need a meal I know I can complete –
A modest buffet, which will never pall,
And will not make me feel I'm too replete.
I think I'll have a sandwich after all!

Envoi

Don't get me wrong, plump Prince, I'm no aesthete,
And yet your bill of fare may well appal;
You say there's soup, roast beef, and then a sweet?
I think I'll have a sandwich after all!

E. O. PARROTT

THE BALLADE WITH TEN-LINE STANZAS

All ballade forms have much repeated rhymes:
Three verses and an envoi bear the same
Old sounds, and these like cliché'd paradigms
Might grate upon the nerves. Much of the blame
Must rest with poets of Provence, whose fame
Has vanished with the years since first they thought
A long verse with refrain might be the sort
Of thing to please the ear. Each stanza's end
Is quite the same, and like a last resort
This sort of thing could drive you round the bend.

It isn't used a lot in modern times;
The free verse school would think it rather lame,
Its constant patter like a pantomime's
Crude doggerel. Most rising writers claim,
Avoiding an existing poem's frame,

That they are true originals, and ought
Not use the rhymes that others use. They're taught
That plagiarism stinks, though all depend
Upon a common language for support –
This sort of thing could drive you round the bend.

Among the well-known versifying crimes
A rhyme that leads is rated high: you aim
To let the words flow freely; mental climbs
To overcome the obstacles, a game
Played out unseen. You subtly try to tame
The metre to conform and not contort
The syntax, whilst not getting overwrought,
But writing in plain speech, as you pretend
It's really prose. Like complicated sport,
This sort of thing could drive you round the bend.

Envoi

And so I will reiterate – in short
There is a ten-line ballade form to thwart
The budding poet, though some comprehend
Its rules and win. But like a battle fought,
It leaves you frazzled – as I can report,
This sort of thing could drive you round the bend.

KATIE MALLETT

THE FIVE-VERSE BALLADE

A Ballade of Growing Desperation

Have you met the Ballade of Five Verses?
    It's a beast that is seldom on show;
The normal type's tough, but much worse is
    A monster permitted to grow.
    No wonder my progress is slow –
        The very idea makes me spit;
    For, my friends, I should like you to know
        When the rhyme-words are doubled, I quit.

You may ask, 'Why these protests and curses?'
    No doubt there's a hard row to hoe,
And the Muse quite unfairly disperses
    Her gifts among mortals below:
    She may dry up entirely, or flow . . .
        She may sit on Parnassus and knit,
    But wherever she chooses to go,
        When the rhyme-words are doubled, I quit.

Though tender to some be her mercies,
    To me they're not commonly so,
For her magic's a version of Circe's
    As worked on Ulysses and Co.
    But those pigs won their lost *status quo*,
        While I in my sty must still sit
    And grunt out inanities – though
        If the rhyme-words are doubled, I quit.

Now, even a hack like me nurses
    Ambitions to glitter and glow –
Provided some donor disperses
    A suitable tribute of dough,
    The reward for frustration and woe,
        The gold-dust that graces the grit . . .
    But unless what he has to bestow
        On the rhyme-words is doubled, I quit.

So out with your bountiful purses,
    You patrons of poets, and strew
Your largesse on this bard who rehearses
    Her skills for your sake – as a pro,
    She's aware that her readers may blow
        Hot and cold as their lordships see fit:
    Give me sunshine and spare me the snow
        And when rhyme-words are doubled, I'll quit.

Envoi

My masters, you cannot say no,
    Since for you I've exhausted my wit,
And I'll tease you no longer, for lo!
    Now the rhyme-words are doubled, I've quit.

MARY HOLTBY

THE CHANT ROYAL

What we, in simple English, call 'chant royal'
   En français, on prononce 'chant royal'.
At once, my blood comes rising to the boil;
   I go outside, unlock my arsenal
And seize a gun for pointing it at Frogs
Who mar the mildest of my monologues,
   So hard the sounds they seek to set my tongue.
   It's all no use: I am no longer young
     And threatening a nation's past my aim.
   My withers now are definitely wrung:
     I'll have to settle down and play the game.

It irks me, when I turn a spit of soil
   And call a spade a spade (I always shall),
That in their *langue d'oc* or *langue d'oïl*,
   Their Basque, Parisian, or Provençal,
These French will train themselves, their poodle-dogs,
Their truffle-hounds, their sheep and cows and hogs,
   The other filthy beasts they live among
   To bark and grunt with all their strength of lung
     Some word like *bêche*. 'Spade' is the proper name!
   All right, I know! My ladder's lost a rung:
     I'll have to settle down and play the game.

In Eire they call the Parliament 'The Dail',
   And run their institutions by cabal;
But though they're generally in turmoil
   I've often called an Irishman a pal.
Leave government, I say, to demagogues;
They all know English in the Irish bogs.
   Even in Scotland English songs are sung;
   I don't believe *all* foreigners should be hung;
     But how can people say that 'cream' is *crême*?
   All right, I know! My barrel needs a bung:
     I'll have to settle down and play the game.

Here is 'chant royal', Prince. If I seem stung,
Remember that my hook will soon be slung;
   And even the Common Market's not to blame
That I am old and rather highly strung.
   I'll *have* to settle down and play the game.

PAUL GRIFFIN

The Porcupine

I bought a single roll of film at Ealing.
I had to ask them where the shutter was.
The Competition sounded quite appealing –
Whilst open to photographers *en masse*,
It had a new 'Beginners' Section' . . . Quite!
(I knew the theory: 'Apertures' and 'Light');
And so for miles around the wonder grew
(That's Housman) as they asked, and asked anew,
'What great *chef-d'oeuvre* will come from this beginner?'
I rose one day at dawn, and in the dew
I photographed a porcupine at Pinner.

'Oh, yes?' you say. 'A porcupine? You're feeling
Unwell, *mon vieux!* Lie down, and it'll pass.'
It passed all right. Through Pinner. It was reeling
With drunken zig-zag movements through the grass.
It came up very close (I thought it might).
It rushed away then. Click! I'd got it right! –
Its message had been, 'Snap me, and I'll sue!' . . .
I think *you* thought I hadn't got a clue
(I think you thought I'd never be a winner) –
My word, you should have seen it as it flew!
I photographed a porcupine at Pinner.

To say that this achievement wasn't sealing
My journalist prowess would be crass.
('Our Nature Correspondent at Darjeeling
Took these fine shots of Bengal tigers, as
The moon, whose rays shone right across the night
Rose upwards, to the Himalayan height') –

Is that a horse of quite a different hue?
My virtues are accounted very few,
My hair on top grows noticeably thinner:
But, though I must admit that this is true,
I photographed a porcupine at Pinner.

The Gobi, and the scimitars are wheeling,
The endless sands are smooth as polished glass
('Our Nature Correspondent, seen here kneeling,
Took this one at f8', and all that jazz).
What, though my teeth are chattering with fright –
I think of what I did, and I SIT TIGHT
(If trembling slightly, like a tree at Kew).
And when the team selectors say they rue
Their nerve in picking me as second spinner,
I say, 'You are entitled to your view:
I photographed a porcupine at Pinner.'

When age and sheer decrepitude are stealing
Significantly near, and what you class
As wisdom of the world is double-dealing,
Or when one goes to Bournemouth for the bass
And has to disembark without a bite
(These things are sent to try us – they are slight),
I piously reflect that there is blue
Behind the darkest of dark clouds. Then, too,
A sense of high achievement's something *inner*:
I shouldn't boast of it, I know – but phew!
I photographed a porcupine at Pinner.

Envoi

Prince, come to give the prizes out, you drew
An altogether wrong conclusion. You
Assumed, sir, in our little talk at dinner,
That I had photographed it at the zoo!! –
I photographed a porcupine at Pinner!

P. I. FELL

*

134

THE DISTICH

The shortest poem: Just two lines, usually epigrammatic.

Dash off two lines of a gnomical distich,
And you'll be mistaken by all for a mystic.

PAUL GRIFFIN

People who live in glass houses
Should watch it while changing their trouziz.

GERARD BENSON

Lines Inscribed on a Wheelbarrow Given as a Wedding Present to Barry and Jo Simner

Two handles drive a single wheel,
So does a happy marriage feel.

GERARD BENSON

There once was a bard of Hong Kong
Who thought limericks were too long.

GERARD BENSON

When epics bore, for light relief
A distich is extremely brief.

KATIE MALLETT

'The proper study of mankind is man.'
Beat that for sheer sexism if you can.

STANLEY J. SHARPLESS

A tea-soaked madeleine consumed by Proust;
Mon Dieu! What recollections *that* unloosed.

STANLEY J. SHARPLESS

We wouldn't blink an eyelid now to learn that he was gay:
Wilde might have got an Oscar if he'd been alive today.

STANLEY J. SHARPLESS

The Viewer's Prayer

Give us this day our daily fix
Of news and sport and porno-flicks.

STANLEY J. SHARPLESS

Helen of Troy

She launched a thousand ships, no less, from little craft to whalers;
You'd say that Helen must have got on very well with sailors.

STANLEY J. SHARPLESS

Pollution

It seems our poor old Planet Earth has had its chips,
Now there's a *Fifth* Horseman of the Apocalypse.

STANLEY J. SHARPLESS

*

THE DECASTICH

What is a decastich?
   Ten lines that are made
     So cleverly they
Make a Brooke or a Flecker stick
   Years at their trade,
     Hoping they may
Distil their fecundity,
   Wisdom and age
Into profundity
   Befitting a sage.

PAUL GRIFFIN

*

THE PASTORAL ELEGY

In English poetry the elegy is a lament, usually in a pastoral setting (see page 139). In classical poetry the term was applied to any poem written in 'elegiacs'; however, in the original pastoral elegies of the Sicilian poets, such as Theocritus, there were strict rules laying down what should be included in each stanza.

Thomas Gray's well-known example of the elegy provides the model for this form in English poetry.

Broadly, an Elegy laments lost things,
    The evanescent nature of us all:
The death of pop stars, puppy-dogs and kings,
    The crumbling marble by the churchyard wall.

The Romans used one metre for the lot:
    Hexameter, pentameter, in turn;
That's fine in Latin, but in English not;
    Read Clough and Kingsley if you want to learn.

It took a Cambridge don to set our pace:
    Gray at Stoke Poges, watching evening fade,
Must have had teardrops streaming down his face,
    So powerful was the Elegy he made.

His feat is hard to equal or surpass:
    But read those stones that block your sickle's way
Next time you try to trim the churchyard grass:
    HERE LIES JIM SMITH, WHO LOVED THE LIGHT OF
      DAY.

Then put your thoughts in quatrains, rhymed like these;
    And to his troops perhaps, to ease their trek,
Some General will read your elegies
    As Wolfe did on the river by Quebec.

But when your job is done, you and your staff
    Who've cleared the docks and lager-cans away
May catch the echo of old Jim Smith's laugh:
    He knows the human mess is here to stay.

PAUL GRIFFIN

A Pastoral Elegy,
According to the Rules

Yet once more, O Melpomene,
A sorrow-stricken dominie
   Entreats the Muse of Hearses
   To insufflate his verses:
Descend, fair maid, *in nomine*
   Of Lycidas and Thyrsis,

> Poem begins with
> invocation to Muse; refers
> to mythological
> characters.

While Nature, keen to master all
True elegiac pastoral,
   With tears makes Tellus muddy,
   Soaks Colin Clout and Cuddie
Whose own laments flow faster, all
   Because they've lost their buddy.

> Nature mourns also.

Their fleecy care, all woebegone,
Bleats loudly, 'Where is Toby gone?
   When mortal danger struck, it
   Was not his way to duck it,
But where was Hodge? Lie low, begone!
   For Toby kicked the bucket.'

> Enquiry into whereabouts
> of guardian of deceased at
> time of death, with rebuke
> for inactivity.

Such taunts may seem obsessional,
But poets are professional –
   We're not here to cut corners,
   Though philistines may scorn us . . .
So next comes the processional
   Parade of diverse mourners:

> Procession of mourners,

If I don't strive to mention all
Their names, that is intentional,
   For creatures tame and woolly
   I can't distinguish fully –
I *try* to be conventional
   So critics, please don't bully!

> preferably identified.

Of right procedure sensible,
I next find indefensible
   Heaven's mockery of justice;
   The cause of my disgust is
That fate incomprehensible
   Put Toby where the dust is.

Reflection on the inscrutability of divine justice.

While hirelings are available
Wild wolves roam unassailable,
   Lean lion prowls, and leopard,
   And harmless birds are peppered;
The whole world's state is wailable
   When sheep have lost their shepherd.

and contemporary evils.

We scribblers fondly sigh, 'O let
Sweet villanelle and triolet
   Be sung where he reposes,
   And, dear to questing noses,
Bring dogwood and dog-violet,
   Dog-parsley and dog-roses.'

Descriptive passage: flowers decorating bier, etc.

Beneath them, scarce detectable,
Lies Toby (it's respectable
   To log this immolation);
   From animate creation
Grim Death is undeflectable,
   But, happy transformation!
Our Toby's resurrectable –
   A canine constellation.

Renewal of hope and joy. Apotheosis of deceased.

MARY HOLTBY

*

GHAZAL

Two definitions of this interesting form (pronounced 'gazzle') are available: we have tried to accommodate both and hope that the result will not offend either party.

1. A Moorish form, probably the origin of the sonnet: short, rhymed ode of fourteen lines, usually with an erotic theme; a love song.
2. Persian and Arabic form: not more than eighteen couplets, the first two lines rhyming together and every even-numbered line thereafter; mainly amatory and bacchanalian.

Broach the barrel, let us guzzle—
Fear not, comrades, that the fuzz'll

Interfere; when on the razzle
We abandon mask and muzzle!

Here the jolly sounds of jazz'll
Bring us girls to hug and nuzzle:

Blissful Bess will have her Basil,
And be sure that all he does'll

Fail to fray him to a frazzle.
Giving other dames the buzz'll

Swell the numbers we can dazzle—
Modest maid and kissing coz'll

Melt to hear our glorious ghazal,
Now its nature's not a puzzle.

MARY HOLTBY

*

THE GLOSE

From the Spanish *glosa* form, this begins with a short stanza, each line of which then appears as the last line of a subsequent stanza, and is explained or developed – 'glossed' – by it.

Texte

Iberians, when overcome
　　With love for some mantilla'd maid,
Will sing a glose *ad libitum*
　　To serve her as a serenade.

Glose

Although the heat is very strong
　　In parts of Portugal and Spain,
A person cannot love for long
Without expressing it in song
　　Not once, but twice, and then again;
It even can be wearisome
　　To hear a man in obvious strain
　　Doing his best to entertain;
But no one says that they are dumb,
Iberians, when overcome.

Do they not dance? I hear you say:
　　Flamenco is the Spanish style;
It surely is the classic way
To celebrate a trysting-day.
　　Yes, yes; but don't be puerile:
You'd have to call the Fire Brigade
　　After a very little while,
　　The midday heat being simply vile,
If you fandango'd in the shade
With love for some mantilla'd maid.

Not wishing to be soaked with sweat
  Or burnt with unrelenting blaze,
The Spanish male, not beaten yet,
Clicking perhaps a castanet,
  Will set his tongue to turn a phrase,
And out of his delirium,
  Fanning his passion with a gaze
  Upon his lady, that conveys
The reason for his martyrdom,
Will sing a glose *ad libitum*.

II

I am not Spanish, Heaven knows:
  Cordoban bulls I cannot chase;
But even so, I can compose
In honour of my love, a glose
  To bring a sparkle to her face:
The song that I have here essayed,
  Sung in a tenor or a bass
  I hope may find an honoured place
With other music I have played
To serve her as a serenade.

PAUL GRIFFIN

*

THE KYRIELLE

Short for 'kyrie eleison', the kyrielle consists of eight-syllable lines arranged either in couplets or in quatrains rhymed *aabb*, with a refrain, which may form part or all of the final line of each stanza.

> The Kyrielle was once a kind
> Of hymn. In fact you'll often find
> Its form in certain liturgy.
> It's loved for its simplicity.
>
> The last line forming a refrain,
> It's easy to intone; the brain
> Can grasp its rhythm easily.
> It's loved for its simplicity.
>
> Its lines are short, each one a set
> Of four iambic feet, and yet,
> Like those who seek a Deity,
> It's loved for its simplicity.
>
> And secular librettists too
> Have used the form; though it is true
> For some it plods too stolidly,
> It's loved for its simplicity.
>
> (Though Coward and Lloyd Webber might
> Have chosen complex forms to write,
> By novices in prosody
> It's loved for its simplicity.)
>
> And when life seems a complex maze,
> For those who love to pray and praise
> The Kyrielle will always be
> Well loved for its simplicity.

KATIE MALLETT

Kyrielle of a Thousand Kisses

Da mi basia mille, deinde centum,
Dein mille altera, dein secunda centum,
Deinde usque altera mille, deinde centum.
Gaius Catullus

Fie, Love. The thing that we would do,
Catullus and his Lesbia knew;
Come to my waiting arms, sweet Lily:
    Da mi basia mille.

For, if Catullus knew his stuff,
A thousand kisses aren't enough,
So I implore you, willy-nilly:
    Da mi basia mille.

Lovers since Eden's time, I wist,
Have toyed and flirted, touched and kissed,
From Tonga to the Ilse of Scilly:
    Da mi basia mille.

And nowadays it's often said
Under the neons green and red
That so enliven Piccadilly:
    Da mi basia mille.

At all the best Hunt Balls, you know,
One hears the cry, 'Yoicks! Tally-ho!
Come over here, you gorgeous filly:
    Da mi basia mille.'

It must, of course, remain in doubt
Whether Victoria would shout
To Brown, her ever-faithful ghillie:
    Da mi basia mille.

Yet sure I am that Abelard
And Eloise (whose fate was hard)
Whispered, although the night grew chilly:
    Da mi basia mille.

And Irish tenors too, I ween,
Have murmured to a fair colleen
Oft, in the night that Moore called 'stilly':
    Da mi basia mille.

At the *Moulin*, proud English earls
Have thus persuaded can-can girls
In frothing undies, wild and frilly:
    Da mi basia mille.

So we, my love, our supper done,
May now enjoy some Roman fun,
In spite of onions and Caerphilly:
    Da mi basia mille.

GERARD BENSON

*

THE ODE

The Greek ode originated with Pindar in the fourth century BC and was written for choral performance. There were three stanzas, the strophe (spoken while moving up one side of the stage), the antistrophe (spoken while moving down the other side) and the epode (spoken facing the audience). There was no fixed rhyming pattern at all, except that the scheme of the first three stanzas had to be followed throughout.

Later, Horace (65–8 BC) devised an ode using just one, freely constructed, stanza as the pattern for all the rest. Keats used this form but developed a ten-line stanza in iambic pentameter – except the eighth line, which was in iambic trimeter – rhymed *ababcdecde*.

HORATIAN ODE

To Keats's Pattern

Oh Horace, Latin lyrist, on your wings
I lift this brief citation. In this mode
As to a bird that through all crises sings
I'll raise my pen in tribute, gladly owed.
Although the civil service occupied
Your working hours, you found a poet's fame.
A friend of Brutus, losing all you owned
By joining the wrong side
You still retained your dignity and name,
At last as Poet Laureate enthroned.

Your phrases are remembered through the years;
Like gathered tax they gain an interest.
Your verse forms have transcended the frontiers
Of language and ideas: they stood the test
Of resurrection by the likes of Keats.
Horatian Ode, as regular as time –
Like clockwork it goes round in equal parts –
Its stanza form repeats,
Its frequency evoking like a chime
The place where labour ends and pleasure starts.

KATIE MALLETT

*

THE PANTOUM

In this verse form, the second and fourth lines of each stanza become the first and third lines of the next stanza, and so on until the *a* rhyme of the first verse is reached again in the final stanza.

The form called a Pantoum derives from Malaya,   *a*
   Where strange Orientals regard it as magic: *b*
It's a fiendish game to be played by one player,   *a*
   Dramatic, satirical, comic or tragic.   *b*

Where strange Orientals regard it as magic,   *b*
   The practice of poetry takes some weird forms: *c*
Dramatic, satirical, comic or tragic –   *b*
   All sorts of ideas that diverge from the norms.   *c*

The practice of poetry takes some weird forms: *c*
   Even I feel the urge to be putting on paper   *d*
All sorts of ideas that diverge from the norms,   *c*
   That madden, provoke and dissolve into vapour.   *d*

Even I feel the urge to be putting on paper,   *d*
   Of all these abstruse and remote sorts of verse   *e*
That madden, provoke and dissolve into vapour,   *d*
   A form like a drug that brings madness or worse.   *e*

Of all these abstruse and remote sorts of verse   *e*
   The form called a Pantoum derives from Malaya –   *a*
A form like a drug that brings madness or worse: *e*
   It's a fiendish game to be played by one player.   *a*

PAUL GRIFFIN

*

HMS Pantoum

Just clear the decks and give me room;
I hear the awful cannon bray!
The flagship, HMS *Pantoum*,
Is now at anchor in the Bay.

I hear the awful cannon bray.
('The foremost of the English fleet
Is now at anchor in the Bay,'
I hear the *boom-crack-booms* repeat.)

The foremost of the English fleet,
She'd hardly left the harbour bar!
I hear the *boom-crack-booms* repeat
From where the fifteen Frenchmen are.

She'd hardly left the habour bar,
The sea was smooth, the weather fair.
(From where the fifteen Frenchmen are
A cannonade has rent the air!)

The sea was smooth, the weather fair –
How swiftly was our ship becalmed!
A cannonade has rent the air –
The Admiral is not alarmed.

How swiftly was our ship becalmed –
This cannot be allowed to be!
The Admiral is not alarmed,
'We'll whistle for a wind,' says he.

'This cannot be allowed to be!'
The Admiral displays no fear.
'We'll whistle for a wind,' says he.
'WE'LL GET TO BLAZES OUTTA HERE!'

The Admiral displays no fear –
A wind is rising on the lee!
(We'll get to blazes outta here –
She's heading for the open sea!)

A wind is rising on the lee!
Just clear the decks and give me room:
She's heading for the open sea,
The flagship, HMS *Pantoum*!

P. I. FELL

*

THE RONDEAU

A form of lyric poem originating from early sixteenth-century France. Its fifteen lines are divided into three stanzas, consisting generally of five, four and six lines respectively, and taking a phrase or word from the first line to use as a refrain to end the second and third stanzas.

The ten-line variation of the rondeau is divided into two stanzas with the opening word of the poem tacked on to the end of each verse as a refrain.

The Deuce, to do his Bad Deed of the Day,
Prepared to lead some innocent astray;
Inspired a so-called friend to challenge me
To write a Rondeau. 'For a bet,' said he.
'You're on,' I said, and started straight away.

The thing was – what on earth was it to say,
This fifteen-liner: easy – mere child's play?
And then it turned out unexpectedly
    The deuce to do.

Its end is its beginning. That's OK,
Perhaps, for starters. But, to my dismay,
I've plagiarized a line of T.S.E.
I give it up. By now, I hope you'll see
It is (I will repeat it, if I may)
    The deuce to do.

JOYCE JOHNSON

In shortish poems like rondeaux
Thoughts are tied up in a bow:
There, loose ends never will be found
Because, to be kept neat and round,
They're clipped, like bonsai, as they grow.

They're not allowed to spread, and so
Ideas cannot take root below
their little piece of potted ground,
In shortish poems.

But they may stay, when others go,
In the mind; like a rainbow
Their structure's airy, yet it's sound:
By changeless laws its shape is bound;
Some poets speak more than they know
In shortish poems.

MARGARET ROGERS

A Thespian Rondeau

'Edmond is dead, my lord' – that was my line
(In *King Lear*, Stratford, 1949).
Although I didn't have to learn a lot.
The line is quite important to the plot,
And Larry told me I was 'just divine'.

I was First Messenger; made the part mine.
In tights and jerkin, suavely Saturnine,
I gave my reading everything I'd got:
    'Edmond is dead, my lord.'

I'd have preferred a line more sapphirine –
'The multitudinous seas incarnadine'
Rolls on the tongue (that's from the 'nameless Scot').
But still I thank the Lord above for what
He once allowed: a draught of vintage wine,
    'Edmond is dead, my lord!'

GERARD BENSON

Perhaps it will be sweet, this by and by;
    Perhaps by then I'll even understand
    Why bird in bush was never bird in hand;
Perhaps that far-too-long-awaited pie
Will cease from floating aimless in the sky
    And land up on my plate, and still taste grand –
        Perhaps!
Perhaps those quaint proverbial pigs will fly,
    My airy castles stand on solid land,
    And I will be a famous poet and
This ten-line rondeau catch a reader's eye –
        Perhaps!

JOYCE JOHNSON

*

THE RONDEAU REDOUBLÉ

This verse form begins with a quatrain rhymed *abab*, the four lines of which are repeated in turn as the final lines of the four ensuing stanzas. The final quatrain, also rhymed *abab*, uses new material, but part of the first line of the first stanza is appended as a final refrain.

When you have done a Rondeau and Rondel
    And you are battered by the storms of praise,
Sit down and weave an even stronger spell,
    Turning your pen to unaccustomed ways.

On the Rondeau *Redoublé* set your gaze:
    A wind of verse that sings like Philomel,
Catches and blows your fancy to a blaze
    When you have done a Rondeau and Rondel.

Its notes chime slowly like a passing-bell,
    Then dance and pirouette like coryphées,
Till all will swear it is a nonpareil
    And you are battered by the storms of praise.

Be firm of purpose, though the world dismays,
    And poets take the easy path to Hell
(I fear not many of them nowadays
    Sit down and weave an even stronger spell).

Mix your Rondeau *Redoublé* very well,
    As strong and saucy as a mayonnaise
Yet delicate and fragrant as Moselle,
    Turning your pen to unaccustomed ways.

Rouget de Lisle once made the Marseillaise
    And gladdened his revolting clientele;
You too will be bombarded with bouquets,
    Though you be modest as the shy gazelle,
    When you have done.

PAUL GRIFFIN

The rondeau *redoublé* is hard to write,
With just two rhymes to choose from for each line.
I'll slog away, and stay up half the night,
And hope the end-result will turn out fine.

The poem has a rather quaint design,
The rhythm's supple and the content's light;
The first four lines will later intertwine –
The rondeau *redoublé* is hard to write.

Average readers, if they're feeling bright,
Four crafty repetitions can divine,
But this strict structure hinders Fancy's flight,
With just two rhymes to choose from for each line.

I'll need some really helpful anodyne,
And though on no account must I get tight,
Well-fortified with Scotch, or maybe wine,
I'll slog away, and stay up half the night.

Although my message may seem rather slight,
This is my hour, and I intend to shine:
I'll give my all (does this sound rather trite?)
And hope the end-result will turn out fine.

When critics mutter, 'What a load of shite!'
I will not dub them interfering swine;
I'll modestly confess, as well as I might,
'It is a paltry-thing, but it is mine!'
The rondeau *redoublé* is hard.

E. O. PARROTT

*

154

THE RONDEL

The rondel is a lyric poem of thirteen or fourteen lines that has two rhymes, usually rhymed *abba abab abbaab*, but there are variations to this. In the fourteen-liner the first two lines become the refrain, used three times altogether, sometimes with variations. The thirteen-liner omits one or other of the two lines of the final refrain.

The rondel's a fourteen-line form,
And two of its lines are repeated –
A bit like a chorus that's greeted
With joy as the listeners warm.

Though only two rhymes are the norm
It sounds pretty neat – when completed
The rondel's a fourteen-line form
And two of its lines are repeated.

When needing a verse to perform,
And epic stuff leaves you defeated,
Exhausted, or just overheated,

To ride out the verse-speaking storm,
The rondel's a fourteen-line form,
And two of its lines are repeated.

KATIE MALLETT

Breathe deeply, and then
  Write down a Rondel;
Settle down in your den,
  Prepare yourself well,

And lift up your pen.
  I know you can't spell,
  But *do* it, pell mell:
Breathe deeply, and then

Try not to rebel;
Though you cluck like a hen
    And you're wanting to yell
And you feel about ten,
Breathe deeply, and then
    Write down a Rondel.

PAUL GRIFFIN

*

THE RONDELET

        Anybody
Can write an airy rondelet.
        Anybody
(past the stage of reading Noddy)
Can cook one up — no sweat —
But never one that has, as yet,
        Anybody.

JOYCE JOHNSON

Rondelet at 7 a.m.

        I can't get up . . .
Not yet. It would be suicide.
        I can't get up.
I haven't had my morning cup
Of tea. It's far too dark outside.
And then there's Kate, my lovely bride!
        I can't get up.

GERARD BENSON

*

THE CHAUCERIAN ROUNDEL

This form is derived from the rondel and is rhymed *abb aba abba*, using two rhymes, with the first line repeated in the second and third stanzas as a refrain.

> A scriveyn bent on ribaudye
> Might choose a roundel to contain
> His comedy, with a refrain,
>
> An ancient form of prosody
> As used by Chaucer, in the main,
> A scriveyn bent on ribaudye.
>
> Though tales of lust and bastardy
> Go on and on, this rhyming chain
> Can spread his wit, like seeds of grain –
> A scriveyn bent on ribaudye.

KATIE MALLETT

Chaucerian Roundel of the Demented Rhymester

Why should I want to find a rhyme for 'orange'?
Others, I know, have tried before and failed;
Through every rhyming dictionary I've trailed.

I sit here, feeding from my little porringe-
R, writing lists of words that rhyme (like 'flailed');
Why should I want to find a rhyme for 'orange'?

Though I'm insured for Act of God, and/or Inj-
Ury, I'm not sure if my mind's entailed . . .
I think I'm going mad . . . my brain's derailed!
Why should I want to find a rhyme for 'orange'?

GERARD BENSON

*

When I walk the Pilgrim's Way,
Ghosts of Knight and Nun and Reeve
Ride beside me, I believe.

Still the lark of Chaucer's day
Carols of an April eve
When I walk the Pilgrim's Way.

Pilgrims on the way to pray —
Are these fantasies I weave?
Call me, if you like, naïve
When I walk the Pilgrim's Way.

JOYCE JOHNSON

*

THE ROUNDEL

The roundel was devised by Swinburne from the rondeau. A lyric poem
of eleven lines, rhymed *abab bab abab*, the first part of the first line is
repeated as a refrain to form the fourth and eleventh lines. As an
alternative, the refrain can be unrhymed.

A Mongolian Roundel
(Written with a little help from Coleridge)

In Xanadu did Kubla Khan a stately pleasure-dome decree
Whose walls and towers were girdled round with chaffy grain (as in a
    barn).
A damsel with a dulcimer he saw beside a sunless sea
    In Xanadu, did Kubla Khan.

She was an Abyssinian maid, with grey eyes (like a mountain tarn, But
    flashing eyes) and floating hair decked out with spots of greenery.
'Beware! Beware!' she cried – and (with a deep descent to bathos)
    'Garn!'

She wove a circle round him thrice beneath an incense-bearing tree;
She fed on honey-dew the while she still twanged out an air by Arne.
He breathed, 'Your symphony and song to deep delight are winning me
    In Xanadu,' did Kubla Khan.

P. I. FELL

*

SAPPHICS

Named after Sappho (seventh century BC), who first devised them,
Sapphics are usually unrhymed, but can be rhymed: not easy in English.

> Sappho, poet, she of the island Lesbos,
> Shaped a stanza which eschews rhyme but uses
> Pairs of trochees sandwiching one gay dactyl –
>   Three times repeated –
>
> Followed by a pithier fourth line, placing
> Dactyl, trochee (one of each) riding tandem.
> Known afar for loving her girl disciples,
>   Was she a lesbian,
>
> Or, from tall Ionian cliff-top falling,
> Did she die a hetero, mad for handsome
> Boatman Phaon? Scholars reject this twee, too
>   Bitter-sweet ending.

TOM AITKEN

*

Song-writer Sappho, she whose fame is timeless,
Ardently penned in quantitative metre
Poems arranged a bit like this, but rhymeless,
Possibly neater;
Hard, though, her feet for English bards to follow –
In such strange rhythms none with safety traffics;
Classical scholars simply have to swallow
Sassenach Sapphics.

MARY HOLTBY

*

THE SESTINA (UNRHYMED)

Technical note   Like a green pig, the sestina is a strange animal. What matters is not the rhymes but the distribution of the *end-words*. The same six appear, in a different and predetermined order, in each of the first six stanzas. Looking back to the end-words of the immediately preceding stanza, you alternate: bottom line, top, bottom but one, top but one, and so on.

The final stanza consists of three lines ending with the originally *even*-numbered end-words (lines 2, 4 and 6); whilst the *odd*-numbered end-words, lines 1, 3 and 5, appear *inside* those same three lines. Got that? *Sestina lente.*

A Sestina of Porcine Verdancy

I chanced to see a small viridian pig:	1
His features, I could see, were strangely verdant!	2
I saw him go, observing where he went:	3
His features (I repeat) were really green.	4
When *he* had gone, there came along another,	5
Viridian, like the first, but not as little.	6

I stood entirely still, and then the little –   6
You take my point, I'm sure – the *smaller* pig;   1
You'll not confuse him, will you, with another   5
Who, larger than the first, though just as verdant,   2
Resembled in his features (which were green)   4
The one whom I refer to? When he went,   3

I tried to work it out, and . . . (*Which* one went? 3
You ask me that? I've told you once. The little,   6
The more diminutive of those two green   4
Porraceous passers-by, the smaller pig.)   1
His features, though they certainly were verdant,   2
Were not alone so. Greenness in *another*   5

Could plainly be observed! (I say 'another' –   5
I mean the second of those two that went   3
Neurotically by. Though both were verdant,   2
The first – you will recall – was rather little,   6
The second was a somewhat larger pig.   1
The features of them both were very green.)   4

I worked it out. The *reason* they were green   4
(The little pig, I speak of, and another   5
Who definitely was the larger pig –   1
He flashed upon my field of view, then went   3
As, bit by bit, I worked it out): a little   6
(Or Lilliputian) pig goes really verdant;   2

A large (or Brobdingnagian) pig goes verdant;   2
The features of them *both* go very green   4
Through eating rather more than just a little.   6
For one thing starts it off, and then another   5
Will lead them on the way that those two went: 3
Excesses of nutrition make a pig –   1

An 'overdo-the-truffles' pig – go verdant,   1/2
So that is why those two went very green!   3/4
(That big one, and another. *He* was little . . .)   5/6

P. I. FELL

Old forms of verse in sheeted darkness stand   1
Like ghostly monuments to fashions past;   2
The feathers drifting in the Muse's house   3
Cover old feelings which have waited years   4
Immobile, needing masters not yet born   5
To bring their ancient furniture to life.   6

Whole centuries of change have drawn the life   6
Out of these forms; what modern readers stand   1
Fashions that died before their world was born?   5
Great poets made sestinas in the past,   2
But now their magic, dusty with the years,   4
Awaits rebirth inside Erato's house.   3

Come, I will step undaunted in that house   3
And try to bring that beauty back to life,   6
Hoping that out of all these countless years   4
One shining form will shed its dust, and stand   1
No longer prisoned in the silent past,   2
But for another era newly born.   5

In medieval Provence it was born   5
And sung by troubadours in many a house;   3
It sang of love, of music, of the past,   2
Of all the coloured purposes of life.   6
Dante's and Petrarch's great sestinas stand   1
As high examples from those distant years.   4

Love is not swallowed by the greedy years: 4
The son of Venus once for all was born   5
And lives immortal, while the mountains stand   1
And planets gravely dance from House to House.   3
Once in sestinas love's abundant life   6
Was chronicled; but that was in the past.   2

Now once again I call upon that past   2
To rise in glory, to throw off its years   4
And stand before us in abundant life   6
Here in one form in which it first was born –   5
A shape beneath the sheets within the house,   3
One of the many that expectant stand.   1

For though they stand all dusty with the past   1/2
Within that house that represents the years,   3/4
They can be born again and brought to life.   5/6

PAUL GRIFFIN

*

THE SESTINA (RHYMED)

Having absorbed and understood the intricacies of the unrhymed sestina, you probably thought that a rhymed sestina was an impossibility. Not so: Swinburne wrote a number, with alternate stanzas rhymed *ababab* and *bababa*. He numbered his end-words 1–6 and then devised formulae for each of the successive stanzas. It is this system that Katie Mallett has used for her poem.

If you can grasp the way this verse is made   1
You'll have a kind of logic in your brain.   2
It isn't only rhymes that are relayed   3
But also final words are used again,   4
And at the end another trick is played –   5
A verse with 'inner words' – let me explain.   6

You'll have to bear with me whilst I explain   6
The workings of the poem, how it's made.   1
Some features I must show to you again,   4
The words that are repeated are relayed   3
In changing order, to confuse your brain,   2
Like chess that needs attention when it's played.   5

But as in a formation it is played   5
Its order will be seen as I explain.   6
At first Sestinas were not rhymed, but made   1
In blank verse, with the last words used again.   4
But rhyme makes a Sestina, when relayed,   3
Melodious and pleasing to the brain.   2

163

For six whole verses beating on the brain 2
The same iambic-metre feet are played. 5
You could well dance to this whilst I explain 6
The way that this Sestina has been made. 1
Its patterns, like a reel, go round again 4
Until the total message is relayed. 3

When Swinburne wrote Sestinas he relayed 3
A lasting love of language, as his brain 2
Worked out the permutations that he made 1
His spirit made an effort to explain 6
The joy he found in words, as they were played 5
Like musical refrains, over again. 4

Though some might think it tedious, again 4
The words go round, a marathon relayed. 3
This might be doing something to your brain 2
But soon the final chorus will be played – 5
An envoi, as I earlier would explain, 6
A three-line verse, and this is how it's made: 1

A split is made, two words are said again, 1/4
Just like your brain, two sections are relayed, 2/3
The tune is played. This sample must explain. 5/6

KATIE MALLETT

*

THE SONNET

Most readers of poetry think they understand about the sonnet, but
there is an amazing variety of rhyme schemes, and even the number of
lines can vary. Shakespeare has one of twelve lines, but fourteen is the
norm, comprising an octet (or octave) followed by a sestet, both of which
can be varied by splitting into two quatrains and two tercets. The
original Italian, or Petrarchan, sonnet has four rhymes only, two quatrains rhymed *abba* in the octave, followed by a sestet normally rhymed
cde twice. The sestet often elaborates on, interprets, or even contrasts
with, the sentiments expressed in the octave. English poets, such as

Milton, found these rules irksome because the English language has fewer rhyming words, so they adapted them, using more rhymes and varying the rhyme schemes. Shakespeare changed the form even more, using three quatrains with a different set of rhymes for each, and a final rhyming couplet using a new rhyme. The Spenserian sonnet is closer to the Italian, using only five rhymes but with many variations in the rhyme scheme. There are nearly thirty variations of the sonnet in *The Oxford Book of English Verse*. At the end of this section Bill Greenwell demonstrates just how 'unruly' the sonnet can be.

THE ITALIAN, OR PETRARCHAN, SONNET

'Scorn not the Sonnet,' Wordsworth said; perhaps	*a*
Anticipating somebody's complaint,	*b*
For short of sonnets Wordsworth's *oeuvre* ain't,	*b*
And though a vein of gold he sometimes taps	*a*
For mile on boring mile the poet naps.	*a*
Like him, however, I would strive to paint	*b*
The thing in glowing colours and acquaint	*b*
You, gentle student, with a form that chaps	*a*
Have used for centuries and do so yet.	*c*
Not long nor short, but neatly fourteen-lined	*d*
(Decasyllabic, with iambic stress)	*e*
This – the *Petrarchan* (or *Italian*) kind –	*d*
Divides into an *octave* and *sestet*:	*c*
The former strictly rhymed, the latter less.	*e*

MARY HOLTBY

Take An Umbrella!

Whether skies are grey or blue, the Brit	*a*
Will talk about the weather endlessly;	*b*
Dour next-door neighbours, even, will feel free	*b*
Upon the topic to display their wit.	*a*
This subject of discourse is right and fit	*a*
For each occasion: where would we all be,	*b*

Meeting prospective mothers-in-law, if we – *b*
Come rain or shine – could not depend on it? *a*
Other nations may have sunnier skies, *c*
Higher mountains, birds with flashier wings, *d*
Denser forests, more exotic flowers, *e*
But still their climates lack the sheer surprise *c*
Of summery winter days, autumnal springs, *d*
And *fêtes champêtres* umbrella'd in snow showers. *e*

MARGARET ROGERS

THE SPENSERIAN SONNET

When Spenser wooed the admirable Betty *a*
    He gave his loving words poetic wings, *b*
And like a flock of feathery *amoretti* *a*
    Sonnet is chased by sonnet as he sings: *b*
    One cupid soothes, another's arrow stings; *b*
Sometimes, it seems, she won't, sometimes she will – *c*
    Her wintry heart melts in successive springs, *b*
Through changing seasons he adores her still. *c*
Petrarch and du Bellay fuel his quill *c*
    – He practised sonnets when translating them – *d*
Wyatt and Surrey helped, perhaps to fill *c*
    The lines that praise his 'goddesse', 'tygre', 'gem'; *d*
He found a form: his variation on it *e*
Deserves the title of Spenserian Sonnet. *e*

MARY HOLTBY

THE MILTONIAN SONNET

If as a working poet you resent *a*
The hours you spend just thinking (as you may), *b*
Or wasting time, as philistines would say, *b*
Remember Milton's harsh predicament, *a*

His sight reduced, the candle's transient   *a*
Illumination dim. One horrid day   *b*
He found that he was blind, but to portray   *b*
His fate he wrote a sonnet. Truculent   *a*

At first, then calming down to see things straight   *c*
(Or so to speak), he found this classic form   *d*
Just right to state his case and let it rest –   *e*

That though the world is frantic, those who wait   *c*
May also serve. The centre of the storm   *d*
Is still. But Milton really put it best.   *e*

KATIE MALLETT

THE SHAKESPEAREAN SONNET

The sonnet is a form that's favourite   *a*
With poets who would like to be well known.   *b*
Its size is modest – tailor-made to fit   *a*
Small gaps in magazines, the neutral zone   *b*
Between opposing columns. Yet its length   *c*
Gives space enough to state an argument.   *d*
Although its structure seems to give a strength   *c*
To quite inconsequential stuff – a vent   *d*
For thoughts and feelings, at the end controlled   *e*
By rhymes on every line (though modern bards   *f*
May stick to assonance). The lincs unfold   *e*
A lasting pleasure, and it's on the cards   *f*
The sonnet will be still around when we   *g*
Like Shakespeare have gained immortality.   *g*

KATIE MALLET

The poet's worth his salt that writes a Sonnet.   *a*
PETRARCH composed a number in his time –   *b*
Started with Form, and froze the Matter on it   *a*
('*In* it', I mean, not 'on it', but a rhyme   *b*

Like 'onnet/in it', if indeed it *may*   c
Roughly be called a rhyme, can hardly be   d
Suitable for the lordly *Sonnet*). *a*   c
bab, followed by *cdcd*,   d
That was how SHAKESPEARE wrote. You may have read   e
This, from poet WORDSWORTH's mighty pen: f
'Scorn not the Sonnet' – which is what *I* said.   e
Wherefore, I'll start this Sonnet once again.   f
   For thus, you may remember, I'd begun it: g
    'The poet's worth his salt and writes a . . .' *Done it!*   g

P. I. FELL

*

SUCCINCT SONNETS

A Sonnet, of a Sorte, Addressed to the Casting Directors atte the Globe Theatre, Bankside, on 14th February 1605

(Yes, I know a sonnet's lines are usually longer than this. But who says they can't be this length: tell me that!)

Must, Val-   a
entine,   b
Thy Sal   a
Repine?   b
(Those were   c
Des cris   d
De coeur   c
From me!)   d
That '(Door)   e
"Sir John"' –   f
A bore!   e
COME ON,   f
   Dear heart –   g
A PART!   g

P. I. FELL

168

Air-Raid Warning
(A monosyllabic sonnet)

Though	*a*
Night	*b*
Fright	*b*
Grow,	*a*
No	*a*
Bright	*b*
Light	*b*
Show!	*a*
This	*c*
Law	*d*
Is	*c*
For	*d*
YOU	*e*
TOO!	*e*

NOEL PETTY

THREE UNRULY SONNETS

PETRARCHAN

Still, there are other sonnets to be paged
(And those who swear by this Petrarchan plan),
Which, though it is no different to scan,
And of a common length, is subtly staged
In two distinctive movements that are gauged
At first to raise, to ruffle, rattle, fan
The simple passions of the common man
Until, the foolish fellow quite enraged,
It tries instead to make him feel assuaged.
Now, soothingly, the sonnet changes gear:
The octave over, its alternate rhyme

Is altered, and a sestet – grave, austere –
Resolves the anxious mood. (*Oh, shit a brick,*
Another gremlin's stitched me up this time!)
Petrarchan sonnets have no final kick.

BILL GREENWELL

SHAKESPEAREAN

A sonnet's length is plainly specified
And, as you'll see, is strictly fourteen-line –
A measured strength that few dare undecide
For that would quite pervert the thing's design,
Which none should ever seek to undermine
However hard they twist its basic plot
Or pattern of its noble rhyming-scheme,
For fear they somehow tamper, like as not,
With Love, the sonnet's most recurrent theme.
A pair of quatrains over: now, with luck,
A scrupulous, iambic set of six
Pentameters will wrap it up. (*Oh, fuck,*
Here's line 13 already: such a fix
A sonneteer must often struggle with.)
The very last line waits to take the pith.

BILL GREENWELL

UNRHYMED

A sonnet some complain is out of court,
Refuses to observe the rhyming rule,
Its dissonance designed, perhaps, to cause
Disquiet in the gut. A jilted heart
May be a proper topic. Whether you'll
Persuade yourself that such an effort ought
To be considered kosher, given status,
Depends on taste. A sonnet has its laws,

As England has. Some feel the sonnet's art
Is sacrosanct, that, frankly, one is deaf
If proud to be irregular; a fool
Eschews the rhyme (*Oh, damn and double-blast,*
A furtive scheme's emerged; its apparatus
abcdbaecdfbgefgd *came sneaking past!*)
And here is line 15. That makes me smart!

BILL GREENWELL

*

THE TRIOLET

Eight lines, not three,
And much repetition,
Just two rhymes – *ab* –
Eight lines, not three,
Seems funny to me,
But that's the position;
Eight lines, not three,
And much repetition.

STANLEY J. SHARPLESS

The triolet? A trifle,
   A dish of cream and sponge.
Should you attempt to rifle
The triolet a trifle
Too seriously, an eyeful
   Will greet you as you plunge.
The triolet? A trifle,
   A dish of cream and sponge.

MARY HOLTBY

The Screw's Lament

Since my head's like a nail
And the rest's like a screw
I am destined to fail.
Since my head's like a nail
No screwdrivers avail.
Yet a hammer won't do
Since my head's like a nail
And the rest's like a screw.

GAVIN J. S. ROSS

Shopping: 1990

She buys one pot of jam – and pays by cheque.
It's vulgar now, it seems, to carry cash.
Though other folks are waiting, what the heck?
She buys one pot of jam – and pays by cheque:
The queue's as long as some great Boer trek.
'Now, *where's* that card? I've lost my Biro – dash!'
She buys one pot of jam – and pays by cheque:
It's vulgar now, it seems, to carry cash.

MARTIN FAGG

A Question

What happens to you really gorgeous girls?
    You shack up with the grisliest of chaps.
Why blast your flower of life as it unfurls?
What happens to you really gorgeous girls
To blitz your wits? It's baffling. Perfect pearls –
    For swine! It's some dark Dido urge perhaps.
What happens to you really gorgeous girls?
    You shack up with the grisliest of chaps.

MARTIN FAGG

*

THE VILLANELLE

There are strict rules you cannot misconstrue:
Five three-line stanzas, capped with a quatrain,
With only two rhymes all the poem through.

A verse-form very difficult to do,
And though you may be bored by the refrain,
There are strict rules you cannot misconstrue.

There's quite a lot of repetition, too;
Annoyingly, that's what the rules ordain,
With only two rhymes all the poem through.

The villanelle's a Muse that's hard to woo;
Though you may feel it's driving you insane,
There are strict rules you cannot misconstrue.

Of course, free-versifiers will pooh-pooh;
They never could withstand the fearful strain,
With only two rhymes all the poem through.

A test for any bard, no matter who,
Because – let me remind you once again –
There are strict rules you cannot misconstrue,
With only two rhymes all the poem through.

STANLEY J. SHARPLESS

The villanelle does indeed normally have five tercets, followed by a quatrain, but a few poets have used seven or nine tercets. In theory, the number of tercets can be any odd number from five upwards.

And So I Did

One never, till one tries, can tell
(What one can do, I mean to say) –
I will compose a villanelle!

173

Maybe for years I've been a . . . well,
A 'mute inglorious Milton' (Gray);
One never, till one tries, can tell.

Hand me my lyre! I'll weave a spell
Of silken sound, and as I play
I will compose a villanelle

Sad like a sigh, or like the knell
The curfew tolls of parting day
(One never, till one tries, can tell),

Or like the song an old sea-shell
Sings of some blue Aegean bay.
I will compose a villanelle

Sonorous, like a silver bell.
Or will I? Can I? Anyway,
One never, till one tries, can tell –
I *will* compose a villanelle!

P. I. FELL

Auden and Empson wrote it far too well –
we underlings can truly not compete;
we look up from our dark poetic Hell

to where they're throned in Glory! What a smell
comes from our efforts; limping sock-shod feet!
Auden and Empson wrote it far too well,

the old farm-labourers' song, the villanelle,
they made so modish, *soignée, svelte, petite*!
We look up from our dark poetic Hell

to their sophistication – Philomel
could not have sung more neatly, or more sweet.
Auden and Empson wrote it far too well!

We're tongue-tied with frustration, or we yell.
Bright melody! And we can only bleat!
We look up from our dark poetic Hell,

up to the heights, from our dim, misty dell.
That form can be atrocious or a treat!
Auden and Empson wrote it far too well:
We look up from our dark poetic Hell.

Experts say the *villanelle* was originally a round sung
by farm-labourers (*villa* is Latin for a farm). Popular
in the Middle Ages, the form became fixed in the
sixteenth century.

GAVIN EWART

*

THE VIRELAI

This has two forms, *ancien* and *nouveau*.

The virelai *ancien* is a tricky medieval form of the lai (q.v.), using the same pattern of triplets and having stanzas of a fixed length. An interlocking rhyme pattern is used: the longer lines of the second stanza must rhyme with the short lines of the first, the third with the second, and so on until the last stanza, where, to add to the complications, the short lines must be made to rhyme with the long lines of the first stanza.

In the virelai *nouveau* all the lines are of the same length. The first stanza begins with a rhyming couplet, and these two lines are used alternately at the ends of the succeeding stanzas, as a refrain. Then, at the end, both are used, but in reverse order. Only two rhymes are permitted, but the rhyming scheme is variable, as is the number of stanzas.

In what's called a Lai,
Not much used today,
One sees
In a clumsy way
How the branches splay

On trees.
Nobody will pay
For a Lai, I'd say,
High fees.

PAUL GRIFFIN

THE VIRELAI ANCIEN

A fully-fitted Virelai
Is not a ship of everyday,
    A mere machine;
It sails a complicated way
Past hill and harbour, bank and brae
    And all between.
Its rhymings never go astray:
Like a well-organized strathspey
    Their strict routine
Reveals a careful interplay –
Twelve lines per stanza, let me say,
    Never thirteen.

Two rhymes per stanza can be seen,
But when the short lines intervene
    The rhyme is new;
Emollient as Vaseline
The longer lines slide in between,
    As hitherto
They have in this; their tone, serene
And never violent or obscene,
    Soft as the dew;
So like some barque or brigantine
They sail on placid seas of green
    Or gentle blue.

But as it nears its rendezvous
And sees the port at which it's due
    Across the bay,

The poem dreams of its début
Among the shouts and ballyhoo
  Of launching-day
And finds the rhyme that, *entre nous*,
We thought had faded out of view,
  A castaway.
And, when its voyage is quite through,
This constitutes its final *coup*,
  The virelai.

PAUL GRIFFIN

THE VIRELAI NOUVEAU

A Virelai of Quite Appalling Sportsmanship

The weather could still have a part to
play in this match.
Cricket commentator

Rain that raineth every day,
You could have a part to play!

'Aussies find a length and line.'
We are 26 for 9.
Rain-clouds of a splendid grey –
Scudding, now, across the bay,
Stirring up the spume and spray,
Playing havoc with the brine –
Come a little nearer, eh,
Move a fraction inland? Fine!
Why not venture all the way –
How about it? (What d'ya say,
Rain that raineth every day?)

True, our No. 7 may
Send our Captain back a sign
He is quite prepared to stay
Rooted, like the palm and pine.

177

But . . . may we not, when we dine
At cessation of the fray,
Toast the rains (their telling trait,
Metaphorically, that they,
Coming, cause the sun to shine!)?
Rain – it's just a thought of mine –
You could have a part to play!

Heavy showers . . . the Highland kine,
From the pasture where they stray,
Scamper back to shelter! Hey,
Maybe, rain, you'd leave the Rhine
To production of its wine?
Macerate *our* porous clay!
Are you (asks this virelai)
Going to contribute, pray,
To a halt in our decline?
You could have a part to play,
Rain that raineth every day!

P. I. FELL

SYLLABLE COUNTERS

THE CINQUAIN

Cinquains
Were invented
By the American
Poetess, Adelaide Crapsey.
Crap – see!

V. ERNEST COX

*

THE ENGLYN

Thoughts on the Englyn

The Englyn is a verse that sings in Welsh:
Anglicized it sounds worse;
Thirty syllables, it's terse –
Could be an old bardic curse.

KATIE MALLETT

Prayer for a Perfect Englyn

O Lord, send me thirty syllables please,
In handy lots of ten,
Six, seven and seven – then,
Rhyme lines, two, three, four. Amen.

V. ERNEST COX

*

THE HAIKU

This is a haiku.
Five syllables, then seven.
Then five more. Got it?

STANLEY J. SHARPLESS

To write a haiku
Count seventeen syllables
(Nothing else counts much).

RON RUBIN

A Haiku has flown
Into our cherry, darling.
So please don't look up!

ARTHUR P. COX

Beauty of Japan
Reduced by Western parlance
To banality.

KATIE MALLETT

The geese flew over.
Uplifting sight – which I missed,
Counting syllables.

N. J. WARBURTON

Paradise Lost
(After John Milton)

Don't touch that fruit, Eve.
Oh my God – she's disobeyed!
Cosmic disaster!

STANLEY J. SHARPLESS

THE PUNNED RHYMED HAIKU

Brass bands tend to hum
    Stout tunes down your receiver
If euphonium.

BILL GREENWELL

Naval histories
    Specialize in writing up
Sailors' indices.

BILL GREENWELL

THE CLERIHAIKU

Mate a clerihew
With a haiku – and then what
     Bastard's been begot?

JOYCE JOHNSON

Peter Palumbo
Cries, 'Mumbo-jumbo!' and rails
At the Prince of Wales.

MARY HOLTBY

THE LIMERAIKU

A haiku will do
For a limerick trick, called
A Limeraiku.

ARTHUR P. COX

For Limeraikus
We should use perhaps the chaps
With higher IQs.

JOHN STANLEY SWEETMAN

Why no Eden? We've
To believe it was because
Adam fell for Eve.

JOYCE JOHNSON

Never scorn the frail.
Faerytale. Keats owed his Ode
To a Nightingale.

JOYCE JOHNSON

The Limeraiku
Adds to rhyming jest from west
A sage eastern hue.

V. ERNEST COX

Why Sappho was so
Magically tragical
Men will never know.

MARGARET ROGERS

The limeraiku
Can do a limerick's tricks –
Be brief but rude too.

KATIE MALLETT

'Modern Art', says Sam,
'Is a sham. Pollock's bollocks,
And Warhol's a ham.'

RON RUBIN

'Don't mix,' said Doc Laine,
'Grape and grain. Whisky's risky
Topped up with champagne.'

RON RUBIN

A spy called Montrose
Knows a quite nifty wheeze: he's
A code in the nose.

RON RUBIN

*

THE NAGA-UTA

Longer than Haikus
Naga-Utas can go on –
A form you can use
Till your inspiration's gone.
Alternating lines,
Syllabled five and seven,
Form the verse confines,
But raised with lyric leaven
Naga-Utas hold
A wealth of thoughts and feelings
Like treasures or gold
Contained by walls and ceilings.
They don't have to rhyme
Or have an ordered rhythm,
But it's not a crime
To experiment with them.
(If you've got a lot of time.)

KATIE MALLETT

*

THE NONET

Who knows who invented the Nonet.
some literary wag, I bet,
Set it as an exercise
In triangular guise,

And so it became
A form, a game,
That suspends,
Descends,
Ends.

KATIE MALLETT

Dial 999

Zek, a woman of the Sabine tribe,
Said, 'I'm upset, as I'll describe.
All these chaps came on this raid,
And did things, I'm afraid.
Some girls had real fun,
But I got none;
"You," said one,
"Not rape
Shape."'

E. O. PARROTT

Mystery

That realistic author Tolkien
Said: 'What do my novels all mean?
I fear those fey elven folk
Are only a bad joke;
Yet Gandalf the Grey
Really does pay.
So don't gripe,
Just type
Tripe.'

E. O. PARROTT

Militant fury Queen Boudicca
Fixed scythes to the wheels of her char-
Iot, saying: 'These will cut
Anything that may jut;
They're fine dissuaders
Of invaders.
First-aiders
Can't fix
Pricks.'

E. O. PARROTT

*

RHOPALICS

'Rhopalics' derives from the Greek word meaning 'baton-shaped'. The syllable count increases from word to word in each line. Eliot in *The Waste Land* varied this by making the count increase from right to left and left to right, in alternate lines.

When darkness adumbrates insomnia,
A final beverage apparently
Works wonders – irritant anxieties
Of daytime terminate delightfully
With Bovril's masculine assurances
Or Horlicks' blandishments: alternatives
Are whisky (possibly calorified)
Or fragrant camomile's persuasiveness . . .
So others solemnly pontificate
And, claiming singular advantages,
Each loudly promulgates exclusively
His special remedy; contrariwise,

I frankly recommend insomniacs
To swallow SLEEPIFEX – reliable,
No heating requisite, impervious
To ill-timed natural embarrassments.

MARY HOLTBY

The Waste Land

In London, meaningless modernity
(Tiresias-foresuffered) stifles roots
And cruelly parodies Shakespearean
Propricties. Barbaric modern world!
In bedsits, eveningwards, rebarbative,
Carbuncular, uncultured, randy clerks
Shag lonely, talentless, indifferent
Stenographers. Wallala leia la.
Dry crickets crepitate incessantly.
Hieronymo! Damyata. Shantih. Notes.

PETER NORMAN

*

THE TANKA

Here is a Tanka,
A verse form of benefit
When poets hanker
To express their love, or wit,
But only a little bit.

KATIE MALLETT

Waka (or Tanka)

One of the problems
With the Waka (or Tanka)
Is the fatal ease
Of carelessly transposing
The T and the W.

NOEL PETTY

Our hedge is no more.
Our cherry-tree lies broken,
crushed beneath the wheels
of a great vehicle. It
smells like a petrol tanka.

ARTHUR P. COX

ON THE LIGHTER SIDE

THE CAUTIONARY TALE

This is a light-verse pattern, devised by Hilaire Belloc.

The chief delight of Joseph Smales
Was reading cautionary tales.
He'd savour them like vintage wine,
Enraptured by the four-beat line.
Then, with the book back on the shelf,
He'd even try the form himself.
At first Joe's lines were merely penned
To entertain wife, child, or friend,
But as the habit took a hold,
Our Joseph started growing bold
And spouting couplets just like that,
Amused that he could do it pat.
A quirk indulged just grows and grows,
And Joseph soon abandoned prose.
At home or office, work or play.
The rhyming couplets now held sway.

What's more, within this rhyming freak
There lurked a moralizing streak.
From every mundane deed or fact
Improving maxims he'd extract
In homilies made so much worse
By being couched in rhyming verse.
His son and daughter found the change
Extremely worrying and strange,
But knew that if they made a fuss
Their dad would only answer thus:
'Be quiet! Not another word!
For children should be seen not heard.'
Joe's weird compulsion grew and spread –
I blush at what must now be said –
To every part of married life.
O pity Jane, his hapless wife!
For wedded joys are somewhat marred
When shared with a demented bard.
Soon every relative and friend
Was sent completely round the bend,
Till one by one they slipped away.
So Joseph is alone today.
His job is lost, his home-life wrecked.
His son has joined some pseudo-sect
That bans all contact with his dad.
His daughter's going to the bad,
Residing in a seedy squat
And getting up to God knows what.
And Jane? She's on a long vacation,
In search of rhythmic variation.

Moral

At moments of connubial bliss
Octosyllabics come amiss;
Discard them at the bedroom door,
Or you'll become a thumping bore:
And, rhymed or not, it's never nice
To go round handing out advice.

KEITH NORMAN

The Lady of Shalott
(With acknowledgements to Alfred, Lord Tennyson)

Part I

Long ago, by Camelot,
Was this Island of Shalott.
No – not a place where onions grew,
But where there was a Lady who
Lived within its silent Tower,
Weaving in her private bower.
Nobody in all the land
Had seen her at her window stand,
Because it had been said by some
A curse upon her head would come
If she looked down on Camelot,
And so she thought she'd better not.

However, she was not denied
The sight of goings-on outside,
For, by a happy chance, or thought,
She used her mirror as a sort
Of horizontal periscope.
(This makes the matter clear, we hope.)

We are not told who cooked her meals.
Poetry too seldom deals
With mundane matters of this sort.
Poets do not give a thought
To humble servants, which is sad.
It seems to us this Tower had
A lack of staff. Was it the pay?
Did no one speak to her all day?

And then – reflected in her mirror,
A knight came singing, 'Tirra Lirra!'
It was the handsome Lancelot
On his way to Camelot.
His armour gleamed, his helmet shone,
Here was a sight to gaze upon!

Forgetting everything, the dunce
Flew to the window, and at once
She knew she'd been and gone and done
An Awful Thing! This ends Part One.

Part II

It seems to us a little odd
That no one saw this Lady bod
Leave the Tower and pinch a boat.
No one brought her out a coat,
No one saw her loose the rope,
And, utterly devoid of hope,
Set herself and boat adrift
Clad only in a filmy shift.
Probably, if truth were told,
She simply caught her death of cold
Floating off into the night
Like that, *à la* Pre-Raphaelite.

It could be that no curse at all
Held her in its deathly thrall.
But in those days, a simple curse,
Especially if done in verse,
Was just accepted as a fact.
To question it showed lack of tact.
And so this Lady of Shalott
Unthinkingly believed her lot,
And if foredoomed to quit her Isle,
Why then, she'd do the thing in style!

A pity. Had she had the wit
To manage things with just a bit
More sense, the Lady of Shalott
Might have married Lancelot.

Moral

From all of this, it's been deduced
The Lady's fate was self-induced;
And so the moral of this verse is —
Do not believe in silly curses.

JOYCE JOHNSON

THE CLERIHEW

As originally devised, these verses were about specific people, but many have been based on place-names, lines of verse, titles, etc.

Edmund Clerihew Bentley
Evidently
Intent on fame,
Called the jingle he devised by his middle name.

So if W. H. Auden, instead,
Had invented this verse form ahead
Of E. C. Bentley, the clerihew
Would be called simply – Hugh.

V. ERNEST COX

E. C. Bentley
Quite accidently
Invented this verse form of wit,
And this is it.

ANON.

E. C. Bentley
Was obviously mentley
Disturbed when
    he conceived
    the clerihew
    – almost as
    gaga
As the dolt who devised the Icelandic saga.

MARTIN FAGG

Donne
Is fonne,
But Chaucer
Is caucer.

MICHAEL FOSTER

The poet Martial
Was very partial
To anything in togas or tunics
From matrons to eunuchs.

FIONA PITT-KETHLEY

Highland Mary
Took Burns into the dairy
To see if he was well-built
Under his kilt.

FIONA PITT-KETHLEY

When I was one-and-twenty
I had plenty,
And sometimes had
A Shropshire lad.

E. O. PARROTT

Gerald Manley Hopkins
Kept pacing the corridors at St Beuno's Seminary muttering something
    that sounded like 'Clippety-clippety-clopkins';
It has been asserted that his superiors thought him rather fey
For a J.

P. I. FELL

'Lines Composed a Few Miles Above Tintern Abbey
On Revisiting the Banks of the Wye During a
Tour, 13th July 1798'
Illustrate
That a title
Isn't vital.

BILL GREENWELL

*

THE DOUBLE DACTYL

Sometimes known as 'Higgledy-piggledies', this verse form was
invented in 1951 by the poet Anthony Hecht. The first line is usually
nonsensical and the second consists of the name of the person who is
the subject of the verse. The fourth and eighth lines are the rhyming
lines, and one line of the second quatrain (usually the sixth) is a double-
dactylic single word.

Hickory Dickory
Micromys Minutus
Plucked up his courage and
Climbed up the clock.

One o'clock struck him all
Tergiversatory;
Had it been twelve he'd have
Wound up in shock.

NOEL PETTY

Scribbelly, scrabbelly,
Alfred, Lord Tennyson,
Wrote 'In Memoriam'
Over the years.

Stanzas and stanzas of
Octosyllabical
Lines about life that will
Bore you to tears.

V. ERNEST COX

Xanadu-xanadee,
Samuel Coleridge
Stuck with his 'Kubla Khan'
Thought up a ruse.

Laying the blame on a
Perambulatory
Person from Porlock was
Just an excuse.

JOYCE JOHNSON

Harrowing heroine,
Anna Karenina,
Tired of her hubby and
Feeling the strain,

Bedded Count Vronsky, but –
No joy. She ended up
Unceremoniously
Under a train.

STANLEY J. SHARPLESS

Nopery Popery,
Catherine of Aragon,
Henry discarded her,
(Anne Boleyn next).

Noncatholicity
Wouldn't have come about
Had not our monarch been
So highly sexed.

STANLEY J. SHARPLESS

Tiddely, widdely,
Ernest F. Schumacher
Lauded the claims of the
Decently small:

O for the joys of the
Infinitesimal!
Even more exquisite,
Nothing at all . . .

MARY HOLTBY

*

THE McWHIRTLE

Named after the protagonist of one of the verses, the McWhirtle is a variation on the double dactyl – with the same metrical pattern – devised by American Bruce E. Newling. The differences are these:

1. Both the 'nonsense' word, which begins the first stanza and the single double-dactylic word, which forms the second line of the second stanza of the double dactyl, are replaced by straightforward lines of verse.
2. An extra, unstressed syllable is added at the beginning of each stanza.
3. The metrical feet can 'rove' from one line to the next, adding to the similarity which this kind of verse has to normal speech patterns.
4. Other variations can occur, such as internal rhyming and additional unstressed syllables added at the ends of stanzas.

As you will see from the second set of examples, it is also easy to transform limericks into McWhirtles.

Dear Ann Landers

I'm really disgusted
With Myrtle McWhirtle,
The out-of-work bimbo
Residing next door.
She knows where to find
Herself honest employment
But chooses instead to be
Neighborhood whore.

Point of View
(After J. Patrick Lewis)

Upsetting the apple cart,
Scholar Copernicus,
Ptolemy's rival for
Solar esteem,

Declared that his helio-
Centrical paradigm
Might be regarded
As rather extreme.

Son et Lumière
(After Anthony Harrington)

We're certainly lucky
That Thomas A. Edison
Dreamed up the phono
And also the light;

For thanks to his genius
Electromechanical,
We can read labels
Of records at night.

Quod Erat Demonstrandum

(After Anthony Harrington)

I'm told that the notable
Euclid Geometer,
Galled by a questioner's,
'What is the use

Of studying doctrines
So axiomatical?'
Answered acutely,
'Oh, don't be obtuse.'

LIMERICK VERSION

Overindulgence

Some dear little children
From Collingbourne Ducis
Developed a taste for
The grape and its juice.

They stuffed themselves full
With that wonderful fruit,
Which explains why their skin
Is the color called puce.

Attaboy

A plumber in business
At Southend-on-Sea
Was beseeched by the
Parlor-maid on the settee,

'Be quick with your plumbing,
For someone is coming!'
The plumber, still plumbing,
Replied, 'It is me.'

Carpe Diem

While Titian, the painter,
Was mixing rose madder,
His rosy-rumped model
Ascended a ladder.

Her pose and position
Invited coition —
No wonder that Titian
Quit mixing and had her.

Basse Cuisine

'I'm feeling quite sick,'
Said a newly wed man
Who resides with his wife
In the town of Clonmel.

'It isn't the screwing
That's caused my undoing
But eating an amateur's
Crème Caramel.'

BRUCE E. NEWLING

*

THE EPIGRAM

The epigram's pithy and terse;
And you'll need to polish a bit;
Remember, when penning this verse,
Its four lines must glitter with wit.

E. O. PARROTT

Arriving is great;
And so is leaving.
It's the bits between
That leave me grieving.

MARTIN FAGG

A perfect marriage –
Their qualities merge:
She's the Hard Shoulder;
He's the Soft Verge.

MARTIN FAGG

Why do we talk of 'making' love?
It sounds like some construction kit.
If sex is a sort of DIY,
No wonder our pieces seldom fit.

MARTIN FAGG

*

THE JINGLE

The all-pervasive jingle –
Its rhymes with a swing'll
Alliterate and irritate
And make your nerve-ends tingle.

The ouncy-bouncy jingle
Lets rhymes and rhythms mingle
To advertise and hypnotize
And make the profits ring-all.

D. A. PRINCE

jǐ'ngle . . . repetition of same or similar sounds . . .
>> *COD*

. . . especially where the verses have few poetical claims
>> *Ogilvie's Dictionary*

We called him Tortoise because he taught us
>> The Mock Turtle,
>> *Alice in Wonderland*

A Tortoise taught us Tort. Tort *ought*
    (As Tort is taught) to be
Taught by a Tortoise, as a Tort-
    oise taught *us* Tort. Agree?

P. I. FELL

THE LIMERICK

A limerick's short and it's slick;
Like a racehorse, it has to be quick:
    The front may seem calm
    And cause no alarm
But the end is the bit that can kick.

PAUL GRIFFIN

With a shape of its own it's imbued –
That's the limerick, witty or lewd;
    Two lines, then you oughter
    Have two more, much shorter,
Then one longer that's funny or rude.

E. O. PARROTT

A lady from Southend-on-Sea
Went along to a publisher's spree:
   'I say, d'you like Kipling?'
   Enquired a young stripling.
'Well, I'm game if you are,' said she.

T. L. McCARTHY

'Oh yes, I'm the real pioneer
Of limericks,' said Edward Lear,
   'But I always incline
   To repeat the first line.
Oh yes, I'm the real pioneer.'

FRANK RICHARDS

There was an old monk of Siberia,
Who fancied the Mother Superior;
   Each time she walked past,
   He'd grab at her vast
And exquisitely rounded posterior.

RON RUBIN

Each morning my wife likes to hector me
To have an expensive vasectomy;
   But the Doc says: 'Look, Fred – it
   Just ain't done on credit:
You'll first have to write out a cheque to me!'

RON RUBIN

Nostalgic in old Aberystwyth,
I sat down and made out a list, with
  The names of the rude
  Lovely ladies I'd screwed.
And the chaps I'd gone out and got pissed with.

RON RUBIN

A frigid young lady from Gloucester
Once had an affair on the coucester.
  'She's cold as gazpacho,'
  Complained her muchacho,
'But I'm doing my best to defroucester.'

RON RUBIN

THE EDWARD-LEAR-STYLE LIMERICK

A limerick-writer from Donegal
Said, 'A limerick penned by McGonagall
  Would be highly enthusiastic
  But probably more than a little periphrastic'–
That satirical writer from Donegal.

PETER NORMAN

A Chaucerian Limericke

A miller ther was, an olde codgere,
Who hadde a yonge wyf, and a lodgere:
  By predictyng a fludde
  Thys craftie yonge studde
Hadde the wyf of the codgere to rogere.

PETER NORMAN

There was an old person of Gretna
Who rushed down the crater of Etna
    Screaming 'Someone inside
    Has bartered my bride
And I'm sure it's that maniac Smetana.'

PHILIP A. NICHOLSON

Colonel Sebastian Cutler,
Chopped by his axe-wielding butler,
    Croaked in disdain
    Through the blood and the pain,
'Good God man, you could have been subtler.'

PHILIP A. NICHOLSON

*

THE UNRHYMED LIMERICK

The limerick, rhymeless variety,
Tries to avoid being indecent,
    It chances its luck,
    By not using the word 'damn',
But the mind reads what the eye doesn't hear.

V. ERNEST COX

A person from sunnier climes,
When asked to write verse for the *Telegraph*,
    Said: 'Oh, my! What is wrong?
    When I sing them a limerick
They tell me I've missed out something vital.'

PAUL GRIFFIN

There was a young waiter called Fritz,
Who got himself fired from the Dorchester,
When he spilt (what a berk!)
Chicken soup down the front
Of a lady with rather large hands.

RON RUBIN

*

THE EXTENDED LIMERICK

Though the verse called the limerick's short
Here's one of a similar sort
That someone invented –
Its lines are augmented,
Its scope supplemented
So more spleen is vented
Whilst using its frame for support.

KATIE MALLETT

The Pied Piper of Hamelin
(After Robert Browning)

He turned up in Hamelin, hell-bent to kill
Rats. When he'd killed all he meant to kill,
He asked for his pay,
But they told him: 'No way!'
So, feeling quite stung,
He vamoosed with their young;
'I wish,' said the Mayor, 'we'd called Rentokil.'

RON RUBIN

*

THE DOUBLE LIMERICK

Sheats and Kelley

A romantic poet called Keats
Was the friend of another called Shelley
The modernist both of them treats
Like a very bad pain in the belly:
    For their rhythm and rhyme
    Are seen as old-time,
    And their meaning is plain
    And their sentiment's sane.
Were they crowned in their day for their feats?
The answer is – not on your nelly!

MARGARET ROGERS

*

REVERSE LIMERICK

There is a young lady whose nose
Continually prospers and grows;
    When it grew out of sight,
    She exclaimed in a fright,
'Oh! Farewell to the end of my nose!'

EDWARD LEAR

(*The Reply*)

Said Einstein, 'You should not take fright,
    Nose growth, exponential,
    Has limits essential:
The end won't go faster than light,
One day it will be back in sight!'

ARTHUR P. COX

THE LIMERICK POEM

The Rime of the Ancient Mariner
(After Samuel Taylor Coleridge)

A mariner collars a guest
Oh his way to a wedding, hard-pressed;
    Bewitched and in fear,
    He has to give ear
To the whiskery, wild-eyed old pest.

The seafarer tells him a tale
About a stout ship that set sail
    South, over the Line,
    And everything fine,
Till – Curses! – a force fifteen gale!

An albatross, bird of good luck
(Which looks like a dirty great duck),
    Now shadowed the ship,
    Safeguarding their trip,
Till the mariner shot it, the schmuck.

Problems: the wind disappeared;
Sun-scorched, the lads blamed Greybeard;
    With many a scowl,
    They hung the dead fowl
Round his neck – most symbolic and weird.

The crew were by now crazed with thirst,
And the old sailor knew they were cursed;
    Then on the horizon
    He clapped his mad eyes on
A ship – and his heart nearly burst.

This ship, alas, turned out to be
A phantom. On board they could see
    Death and Death's Mate
    Playing dice for their fate;
The upshot: all perished but he.

Remorseful, he lay on the deck,
A pitiful, gibbering wreck.
    Then he started to pray,
    And the curse flew away –
And the albatross fell from his neck.

Then rain came, and wind like a whip,
And the Dead rose to man the tall ship –
    A skeleton crew,
    But they knew what to do –
And the vessel moved off at a clip.

Well, to cut a long story quite short:
The Fates became bored with their sport;
    They called it a day,
    Sped the ship on its way,
And somehow it limped home to port.

The vessel was now neither spick
Nor span, and it sank double-quick;
    But a pilot's boat raced
    To the rescue, post haste,
And the old salt was saved in the nick.

Now a hermit, who lived in a wood
Near the harbour, was Holy and Good;
    The sailor confessed,
    And the hermit, impressed
Absolved him as best as he could.

Yet still, as a penance, he must
Drift round this planet like dust,
    And make a career
    Out of bending the ear
Of folk, who are often nonplussed.

He exits on uneven keel,
And the guest, though in need of a meal
    And some booze, opts to ease up
    And bypass the knees-up
Which somehow has lost its appeal.

RON RUBIN

THE LIMICK

To involve me in writing this gimmick?
You really must think me a dim Mick.
  A limerick without a third line,
Or is it the fourth? That's the limick!

ARTHUR P. COX

When Lot, through no fault
Of his, had to halt,
  To those just behind
He said: 'Please pass the salt!'

JOYCE JOHNSON

Battle-scarred,
The battered bard
  Backed into
The avant-garde.

RON RUBIN

When a barman called Darryl
Wore ladies' apparel,
  The gov'nor soon had him
Over a barrel.

RON RUBIN

A fellow from Dawlish
Likes girls who are tallish –
  Not Brobdingnagian,
More Lauren Bacall-ish.

RON RUBIN

A dipso called Cooper
Thought Buddha quite super.
    He ended his days
Out East, in a stupa.

RON RUBIN

A Limick Poem

A Limick's so short
That you wouldn't have thought
    You could get very far
In a work of that sort.

Let us face the fact, viz:
Though some Limicks fizz,
    Many others don't finish.
Perhaps the truth is . . .

PAUL GRIFFIN

*

THE BLUES

Hampstead Woman Blues

I've got a gal who lives up Hampstead way,
Yes, I gotta woman, lives up Hampstead way,
And she reads me goddam verse all night and day.

Well, I woke up this mornin' with an awful achin' head,
Yeah, woke up this mornin' with an awful achin' head,
And the doctor told me it must have been that stuff she'd read.

Now I hate to see that evenin' sun go down,
I hate to see that evenin' sun go down,
Because tonight's the night the Poetry Circle's comin' round.

Hampstead woman, you treat me, oh, so mean,
Hampstead woman, you treat your daddy so mean,
Always got your pretty head stuck in a book or magazine.

Well, I love you, baby, but you don't treat me right,
Yes, I love, you baby, but you don't treat me right,
Don't need no poetry, I'd rather drink and ball all night.

Gonna pack my suitcase, move on down the Line,
Pack my suitcase, movin' down the Northern Line,
Gonna get me a new woman, the most lowbrow I can find.

RON RUBIN

THE CALYPSO

Wordsworth Calypso

If Wordsworth had lived in Kingston Town
He'd never have written that sonnet down;
Westminster Bridge is a beautiful thing,
But it needs the Caribbean swing.
    Wake up, London, hear my song!
    London, you been asleep too long!
    And Willyum Wordsworth, he'd be fine
    If only he'd swung the Calypso line.

Now everybody's proud of London City:
In the early morning it's really pretty;
There's majesty in every acre –
It's nearly as beautiful as Jamaica.
    Wake up, London, etc.

That old River Thames is quiet and bare;
There are ships and towers and churches there;
Just leave your breakfast in the fridge
And stand for a bit on Westminster Bridge.
    Wake up, London, etc.

That old man Sun he shines his light
And he makes the whole of London bright;
The calm and the river and the boats are grand
When you give them the rhythm of a good steel band.
    Wake up, London, etc.

Oh, London City to poor old Will
Seemed like a heart that was lying still;
But a heart that's still is a heart that's dead,
So let the Calypso beat instead.
    Wake up, London, etc.

PAUL GRIFFIN

*

OGDEN NASH COUPLETS

I don't see why everybody thinks poetry's such a big deal,
Or why it's supposed to be the only way to say how you feel.
It seems to me a poet is mainly a guy who declines
To write his stuff in the regular way, and insists on doing it in lines.
As for rhyme, metre and rhythm,
These days even the poets don't much bother with 'em.
But you say that to a poet, and he'll soon start to expound
About how it's all to do with sound.
Some will even tell you that a poem can communicate its story in
A language you don't even know, like Urdu or Manchuryin.
If that's the case, anything that gets through has got to be subliminal,
Which, if an adman tried it, you'd call criminal.
It's the same the whole world over, I suppose –
One law for the poets and another for the pros.

NOEL PETTY

THE RUTHLESS RHYME

The remedy I found for Ruth
To stop her drinking liquor,
Was adding lime to her vermouth.
The lime was 'quick' – her death was quicker.

These lines reveal the awful truth – yes,
Both the rhyme and I are Ruthless.

V. ERNEST COX

Mary had a little lamb;
The midwife was upset:
'I warned your Momma that a ram
Is not the ideal pet.'

RON RUBIN

214

VERS DE SOCIÉTÉ

Who Cares What Gentlemen Prefer?

Blondes Prefer Gentlemen
Who answer the phone
And use a butterknife
When dining alone.

ARDA LACEY

SPECIAL EFFECTS

ACROSTIC VERSE

Sir John Suckling

Soft, we should part, my sweeting;
I would forsake the chase.
Rest from thy vain entreating,
Jealousy hath no place
On such a comely face.

Helmsmen must raise their anchor;
Nurslings must cut their strings.
So let us, without rancour,
Use all that Venus brings:
Cupid had ever wings.

Kisses should leave no sorrow,
Love is not made for pain.
If, when thou wak'st tomorrow,
Nostrums are all in vain,
Go, seek some other swain.

NOEL PETTY

DOUBLE ACROSTIC

A Double Acrostic irks me like an irritating fleA:
Consider how you find a word that ends in letter C
Rhyming with one that ends in A! The old vernaculaR
Offered more opportunities nine hundred years agO,
Since French was then predominant, with phrases like *faux paS*,
Tant pis and *droit de seigneur*, *fille de chambre*, and *bon moT*
Inhabiting a language that was like a pot-pourrI,
Causing Double Acrostics to be straight as ABC.

PAUL GRIFFIN

Cuckoo

Cuckoo, cuckoo! the sound is like a tiC
Upon the cheek of day – I blush at yoU,
Crying aloud to every passing fliC:
Killed in the egg is yet another chicK;
Officer, there is nothing you can dO –
Our motto's '*Lebensraum*': cuckoo, cuckoO!

MARY HOLTBY

*

ALPHABETICAL VERSE

An Alphabet of Love and Literature

After an amorous anguish, Art, awake!
Blossom before bard-bitten Biro break.
Converting chaos cheering calm creates,
Deadens despair, displaces daft debates.
Elegant elegies engender ease;

From frantic fevers fruitful Fancy flees,
Gaffs griping griefs, gets grand gestation going:
Harsh heartlands harbour harvests – hasten hoeing!
    Insistent invitation inly irks:
Jests, jingles, jeremiads? Judo-jerks,
Kinky kinetics, kickshaws . . . kissers know
Love lingers, listless literature lies low.
Make me more masterful: my modest Muse
Needs nourishment – *necessity's not news.*
Old overthrows obscure, obliterate;
Prizes possessed, pale poets proudly prate,
Quests querulous, quaint quondam quirks quite quit,
Resume ripe rhetoric, rough rhymes re-fit.
    So – stop such stupid sentimental stuff:
Triumph transforms; true troubadours talk tough.
Up, underdog, urge unity unkenned,
Vanquish vain virgins – *victor's* verses vend.
When wanton woman's won, witty words weigh:
Xerox xenogamy's xenial X-ray . . .*
    Yellow-haired youngling, yield you your yashmak;
Zestfully zig-zag *Zeitgeist's* zodiac!

MARY HOLTBY

*For the ignorant:
xenogamy = cross-fertilization
xenial = pertaining to hospitality
This line might therefore be rendered: Apply the photo-copier to the results of your penetrating analysis (from a friendly viewpoint) of the cross-fertilization you have achieved (see previous line).

*

THE ALPHABET POEM

A Poetic Alphabet

A's for the Accent that falls in each foot,
B is a Ballade with Envoi to boot.
C is a Couplet, two lines, I can't fool yer,
'D is a Dactyl,' says Fowler, 'as *Julia.*'
E's for Endstopping, when sense fits the line,
F is for Free Verse, no shape or design.
G is for Greece, that's where scansion began,
H is for Haiku that comes from Japan.
I's an Iambus, a natural rhythm,
J's just a Joke, what can we do with 'm?
K is for Kanga that's followed by Roo,
L is a Limerick, frequently blue.
M is a Madrigal, sing it in parts,
N is for Nonsense that's dear to our hearts.
O is for Ode or for Onomatopoeia,
P is for Prosody, dismal and drear.
Q is a Quatrain, four lines you'd suppose,
R is for Rhyme that makes verse out of prose.
S is the Sonnet which some think divine,
T is a Triolet, daintily fine.
U's the first blank in poetical parlance,
V is a Villanelle, countryside dance.
But W, X, Y and, finally, Z
Are sadly and surely poetically dead.

JOHN STANLEY SWEETMAN

*

CIRCULAR VERSE

     -ial game that's just the tick-
       et for the gentle Brit-
     isher: that is crick-
       et, against the fit-

               test people in the u-
                 niverse, i.e. the Aus-
                 tralians, all sui-
                 ted in dazzling cos-

tumes of white, while po-
  ets are humbly work-
ing long hours of o-
  vertime to make a circ-

         ular verse, belie-
           ving it's always fresh-
         ly wonderful to re-
         alize there is one spec-

PAUL GRIFFIN

*

DAISY-CHAIN VERSE

In this form of verse the final letter of each line becomes the first letter of the next line.

Poetry – Yes!
Some Encouragement Towards Saner Readership

Poetry yields such heartfelt tears,
Such hopes surrendered, deaths sustained:
Don't trust these elegiac cries
Simplistically – you unfeigned
Delights shall likewise exercise;

220

Expect to open newmade ears,
Shaped deaf for rubbish, hearing gone
Except to offerings sympathetic;
Cheerfulness target the emetic
Charades *some* elegists supplied.
    Drat tears! skip poems sans (*sic*) comic clarity:
    You'll learn new wisdom, mellow with hilarity.

MARY HOLTBY

*

'Echo' Poem

'We're having drinks on Sunday. Can you come?'
      'Um . . .'
'There should be lots of people that you know.'
      'Oh . . .'
'And bring the kids. Or not, as you prefer.'
      'Er . . .'
'Eleven till one; just drop in anytime.'
      'I'm . . .'
'That's settled, then. How's Roger, by the way?'
      'Eh?'
'That is East Grinstead three-two-seven-o?'
      'No.'

NOEL PETTY

Four-Letter-Word Poem

Shun love, wise maid, lest love turn into hate;
When joys leap high, what long dark fall must wait!
Gaze over some fair pool, your eyes will miss
That wood deep down – mean love acts just like this.
Soft lure, base wile, sour trap – list arts more grim;
Each fits this vile name, love; they sink that swim.
When Eros' evil dart aims true, folk reel;
Once made, that open sore what balm will heal?

221

Play ball with love – alas, love wins that game;
Pipe – love will call your tune, your wild note tame.
Free – love will bind your feet; pray, then, poor fool,
Whom fire, when felt, must burn – take heed, keep cool.
Mark well this gate: pass here, love asks full toll . . .
You'd risk your body? Love will have your soul.

MARY HOLTBY

*

INFLATED PROVERBS

He Laughs Best Who Laughs Last

Between the qualities of rival mirth
   There is to be discerned a great disparity;
Priority in time yields place in worth
   When measured against ultimate hilarity.

LESLIE JOHNSON

Fine Words Butter No Parsnips

Felicitous thy utterance may flow,
   With every charm of elocution graced,
Yet no emulsive mutancy bestow:
   The humble root retains its vulgar taste.

MARY HOLTBY

Even a Worm will Turn

In subterranean domicile degraded
   To a downtrodden and supine condition,
Earth's meanest denizen, too oft invaded,
   Effects reversal of his prime position.

MARY HOLTBY

The Proof of the Pudding . . .

Comestibles untested heretofore
   Submit not anxiously to idle question;
Rash diagnosis Reason must deplore,
   Since validation's subject to ingestion.

MARY HOLTBY

A Stitch in Time

A penetrative punctually employed
   To undulate a filament by traction
In singular performance will avoid
   A treble triplication of the action.

MARY HOLTBY

You Can Take a Horse to the Water but You Cannot Make Him Drink

Towards the running stream the sporting gal
   May urge her equine quadruped to go,
But down its alimentary canal
   What human skill can force the H_2O?

JOYCE JOHNSON

You Cannot Make a Silk Purse Out of a Sow's Ear

You can make nothing in particular
   And certainly no pouch of fabric fine,
When landed with the coarse auricular
   Appendage of the adult female swine.

JOYCE JOHNSON

*

MNEMONIC

The Poets Laureate

Look – the Laureates! (We find
Some in front and some behind.)

Hind and Panther – DRYDEN! (Made
To take shelter in the shade.)

SHADWELL. Plenty on his plate.
(Shading pictures for the Tate?)

TATE (he wrote on tea).[1] Hullo –
Tea plantations! row on row.

Rowe? Oh . . . ROWE! (He wrote a play
Tragically, on Jane Grey.)[2]

Grey the areas that EUSDEN
Used to write about, and mused on.

Muse, remember Colley CIBBER? –
Played the ghost and made him gibber.

Gibbous moons (that lighted WHITEHEAD
Plus the other poets cited),

Sighted ye a WARTON, T.?
(Warton's Works – where can they be?)

Be upstanding, Henry PYE:
πr^2 means – what, and why?

Why, it's SOUTHEY! (Guy remains
Unconvincing, on 'Who gains?')[3]

Rains on high Helvellyn make
WORDSWORTH huddle by the lake.

Lake contains a samite mitt.[4]
(TENNYSON's observing it.)

Observations down the wire.[5]
(AUSTIN, what poetic fire!)

224

Fires that flash across the ridges
Light up his successor, BRIDGES.

Bridges? MASEFIELD on them. (He
Had a feeling for the sea.)

C. DAY-LEWIS followed. (Mark
How he kept us in the dark.)[6]

Architectural *élan*,
Great construction. BETJEMAN.

Man of wildwood, now. (We've got
HUGHES today.)

And that's yer lot.

P. I. FELL

[1]This is entirely accurate information. Nahum Tate wrote 'Panacea: a Poem upon Tea'.

[2]*The Tragedy of the Lady Jane Grey* (1715).

[3]'But what good came of it at last?'
Quoth little Peterkin: –
'Why that I cannot tell,' said he,
'But 'twas a famous victory.'
Southey, *After Blenheim*

[4]And arm – brandishing the sword Excalibur.

[5]Across the wires the electric message came:
'He is no better, he is much the same.'
(But let us be fair. Though generally – and plausibly – attributed to Austin, this was 'probably not his', according to *The Penguin Dictionary of Quotations*.)

[6]Until the final dénouement, that is. He wrote whodunnits, under the name of Nicholas Blake.

*

MOPE POEM

If OVER all the world a chap might ROVE
    And TOPE in pubs with every boozing POET,
Would pleas OVERT secure the treasure TROVE
    Or subtle hints inspire the WISH TO SHOW IT?
Ask me to NAME the treasure that I MEAN
    Or if I FARE in hope, or faint for FEAR,
I will confess that my ELAN grows LEAN –
    AERY ambition dreads the coming YEAR.
Yet CHEATS I hate: my Muse shall still stay CHASTE;
    My WORDS alone shall wield the conquering SWORD
If I attain that STATE I long to TASTE
    As DRAWER of *In Print*'s supreme REWARD . . .

A year of downs OR UPS? Dries she, or POURS
POETIC STORM 'gainst all COMPETITORS?

MARY HOLTBY

*

226

NONSENSE VERSE

I prume to be a plomby-headed mard
And yet, reflunging all my connonstatz,
I have this yerkish, werly-making blenk;
In cort, I am a bibbledoop for cats.

They snarge my trousers, croodle on my desk,
Infittie all their izzies on my lap
And, moon-bedimbled, yargle by my bed
Despite their costicarpered catout flap.

In spring their randling fanticates the lawn
And prowky Toms enmax their turby thews;
Then pit-pit into durkling mobby-holes
For nestifur and pids and weely mews.

Once more I scrange the metrodrop for homes
And wonder how I thale this feliblitz –
But, oh, how crack the mowless dute would be!
As glemp as a weekend sans competitz.

ALISON PRINCE

*

NURSERY RHYMES REWRITTEN

GOOSEY GOOSEY GANDER
(Variations on a Theme)

Who *was* it who threw the old man downstairs? The goose? Or the anonymous narrator? I prefer the goose; and so, as you see, did the poets who have tackled the tale over the centuries.

William Shakespeare

LADY MACBETH	It is the goose that honks, the fatal bellman That roams the castle stairs. Hast done the deed?
MACBETH	I was afeared to look on't, for the bird Screamed so, and seized me by my nether limb, Hurling me down upon the cruel flags; And yet I could not pray, nor say 'Amen'. See how I halt; and ever in my ears The gander's fury rings.
LADY MACBETH	And so it shall! I'll wring its neck that it may ring withal! (*Exit*)
MACBETH	She murders creatures as she murders words. Let's hope her cunning does not match the bird's.

Alexander Pope

Male feathered creature, anserine in fame,
Who to a kind of pimple gave thy name,
Speak, and inform us where thy purpose tends,
How wide thy ranging, and how great thine ends.
'I sought to comb this house, inspecting oft
From hall to cellar, and from thence to loft;
But where my lady most prefers to pass
The morning hours in gazing at her glass
An aged heretic instead I found,
Whose leg I seized, and hurled him to the ground;
Whence he proceeded down the stairs to fall,
Bounced on the landing, and attained the hall.'

The flying goose went up the stairs
    And nowhere did he stay;
The flying goose went up the stairs
    And down another way.

Ah, God! I shot that lovely goose:
    I fired without a word –
Which wasn't of the slightest use:
    I missed the cursed bird.

I tried to pray – no use for that,
    I could not say my prayers:
And that is why you find me at
    The bottom of the stairs.

Oh, that is why I rue my lot
    And sing you all this song:
My lady's chamber's *not* a spot
    To linger very long.

John Keats

My leg aches, and a frowsy glumness bears
    Upon my senses, for a great white bird
Has seized my limb, and flung me down the stairs.
    Hark! where the seasonable gloom is stirred
        By omens of tomorrow;
When I must wake and feel the strength of sorrow.

I cannot see the stair up which I went
    Seeking the door to my beloved's cell.
Alas! that there should be such punishment
    For one who loved so longingly and well!
        This is a world of bruising
Where age grows sick, and suffers much abusing.

Where did it go, the vision that I saw?
    The white wings beating ceaselessly above
My questing head, the cruel beak and claw

That hurled me headlong from my lady's love?
No sound the silence breaking:
I am alone, half-sleeping and half-waking.

Alfred, Lord Tennyson

All day within the house the goose
  Went up and down the dreary stair.
My lady sighed: 'It is no use –
  Gander or goose, I do not *care*.'
The goose replied: 'You feel so drear
  Because an old man's in your room.
Until he hears the crack of doom
  He will not say his prayers, I fear.'
    She only said: 'His left leg seize;
      He is the cause of all.'
    She said: 'I shall be more at ease
      When he is in the hall.'

W. B. Yeats

Because I watch the window pane
  But cannot see a thing
I call upon you, royal bird,
  To tell your wandering.
      (A great male goose it was)

'Up and down the tower stair
  Faithfully I've been
And to the holy place where sleeps
  The Countess Cathleen.'
      (A great male goose it was)

'An aged beggar there I met,
  Mad as a windy lake;
I threw him down the stairway
  For old Ireland's sake.'
      (A great male goose it was)

'I threw him by the left-hand leg –
  He would not tell his beads:
And there's an image for the world
  Which the world needs.'
                    (A great male goose it was)

Dylan Thomas

Over the dumbfound stair
The goose hangs in the air
In a hoisted flight, singing the guilt
Of an old man dying of lust,
Foretelling the blood that must
Be spilt;
And his clawed stare
At the ruttish loon
Shows in the light of the mast-high moon
The startled face of him who cannot pray,
The left uplifted leg of the old dog,
The cast-down rogue
That moans on the step for the day
To douse night's fuses
As they burn his bruises.

PAUL GRIFFIN

*

UNIVOCALICS

This verse form uses only one vowel throughout the poem.

Verses re Verse

Ye'd peddle verse? Well, then perpend:
Test the emergence, centre, end;
Let sense be helped, let metre lend
    The needed stress.
Gentleness, vehemence – the blend
    Emends excess.

Ne'er let mere sweetnesses be penned;
Eschew 'effects'; select, extend,
Delete where terseness seems the trend;
    Gentlemen erst
Preferred the deft – feel free, yet bend:
    Ye'll be well versed!

MARY HOLTBY

Five Univocalic Versions of a Famous Lullaby

'A'

Nap, brat, branch fast,
Napsack traps blast;
Branch snap, sack fall . . .
Crash sack, crash all.

'E'

Sleep, pet, where trees crest,
Breeze frets bed rest;
Tree bends, bed descends,
Pet's tree-rest ends.

'I'

Whisht, kid, swing high,
Crib spins if wind shrills;
Twig splits, crib slips,
Sinks crib, kid spills.

'O'

Rock, tot, on top spot,
Storm rocks tot's cot;
Top rots, cot flops,
Cot's down, tot drops.

'U'

Hush, cub, up shrub,
Gusts tug snug bunk;
Shrub's bust, bunk's sunk,
Dumps cub – junks bunk.

MARY HOLTBY

POETIC FANCIES

Some writers of light verse may use a well-known poem, or a famous writer's style, as a springboard for some verse fantasy of their own. Here are a few examples of this.

*

Muse Review
or, as Sir Noël almost said,
A Talent To A Muse

In the throes of verse gestation
Writers seeking inspiration
Should invoke the aid divine
Of the sacred Muses Nine.

Mnemosyne was their Ma,
Randy Zeus their fond Papa;
And each different kind of verse
Has a Muse as guide and nurse.

Tragedy has Melpomene;
Comedy, Thalia zany;
Lyric Poems light and chirpy
Are the province of Euterpe.

If your Epic Verse is ropy
Ask the aid of Calliope:
Polyhymnia – Sacred Chants;
Terpsichore – Song and Dance.

Clio is in charge of History,
Love Songs are Erato's mystery.
Finally, with bonhomie,
Urania does Astronomy.

W. F. N. WATSON

*

On Eighteen Laureates

O Poet, live in glory great, and never be a Laureate,
But shrink in dread from Dryden's fate, who first for Court did cater,
Where Shadwell, Tate and Rowe orate as boozy Eusden bangs his plate
And Cibber clobbers Whitehead's pate while Warton woos the waiter;
Defy the Pye that Southey ate, where Wordsworth's birds of Nature
        prate,
Where Tennyson a-tilting sate, unhorsed by Austin's freighter!
Like Bridges, brave the Traitor's Gate, and swim like him, and bite no
        bait,
Though Masefield, racing up the straight, invites the imitator;
Nor, like Day-Lewis, sublimate from red of dawn to bluish slate,
But blaze and blast in love and hate, O vast volcano-crater!
For those who etch our earthly state, John Betjeman can still locate
And satirize, or consecrate, our land, our Alma Mater . . .

But Oh, in fame and fashion's spate, when Nature grows too passionate,
Can anybody venerate a Dame so unregenerate?
Ted Hughes, we would reiterate, though glitteringly literate,
Could get the Court a *bit* irate; for, if one views his data,
Our Culture must evaporate when all our walls dilapidate

As polar gales at rapid rate gyrate from the Equator:
In Palace and Palatinate, where pikes and cats concatenate,
And horses, sunk beneath their weight, can neither spell nor punctuate,
One cannot but extrapolate on what will happen later . . .

O Poet, choose – consult thy Muse – *refuse* to be a Laureate,
And for a Mandate to create, apply to thy Creator!

GINA BERKELEY

*

A Villanelle by the Poet Laureate

Crow's claws grip the bull-calf in the steading,
His beak tears at white entrails and blood.
I've got to do another Royal Wedding.

A golden bee, after every flower treading,
Settles for life in a pale, sweet, pink-tinged bud.
Crow's claws grip the bull-calf in the steading.

I, Crow, I keep small creatures dreading.
My name is darkness and my brain is thinking mud –
I've got to do another Royal Wedding.

The English rejoice, all living south of Reading,
That the royal stallion has finally gone to stud.
Crow's claws grip the bull-calf in the steading.

A lamb's eye, a rabbit's guts he's shredding, ·
Crow's a waster, destroying like a flood.
I've got to do another Royal Wedding.

Take the salary and do this dressed-up bedding,
Ewart. You've always specialized in writing crud.
Crow's claws grip the bull-calf in the steading.
I've got to do another Royal Wedding.

REM BEL

*

A Dream of 'Kubla Khan' by Sir John Betjeman

In Amersham did Kubla Khan
   A stately pleasure dome decree:
Where Alf, the phantom jogger, ran
Through crescents measureless to man
   Down to a Sunday tea.
And twice five miles were woven round
With London's splendid Underground.
And there were gardens with neat wooden gates
Where blossomed many a fragrant English rose
And here were sandwiches on shiny plates
Amid the coils of a garden hose.

But, oh! that tunnel on the Metropolitan line,
Passing out to air, to Amersham, beyond!
A jolly place! where blue skies ever seem to shine
And where, beneath suburban spires, benign
Ghosts of women wait for curates by the pond.
And from this tunnel, with a heat quite overbearing,
As if the City had its woollen vest been wearing,
A stream of travellers suddenly emerged:
Amid whose bobbling bowler hats there surged
Huge brollies vaulted like the chestnuts in the lane
Because their owners thought it looked like rain.
And 'mid these city workers ran one more fit;
It was the phantom jogger in full kit.
Five miles meandering with a mazy motion
Through merchant bankers the phantom jogger ran,
Then reached the crescents measureless to man,
And sank in steam with a bath-time lotion.
And 'mid this tumult Kubla heard from far
The sound of neighbours washing down the car!

   The shadow of the dome of pleasure
   Stretched across the cricket ground;
   Where was heard the mingled measure
   From commuters homeward bound.
It was a miracle and sure to please,
A sunny pleasure dome with strawberry teas!

A damsel with a cricket bat
    In a vision once I saw:
It was a nice surburban girl
    Who gave her cricket bat a twirl
And joined me for a pleasant chat.
    Could I revive within me
    Her hearty tone of voice,
To such delight 'twould win me –
Oh, my lovely, splendid Joyce –
I would build that dome in air;
That sunny dome! That white marquee!
And all who heard should see them there,
And all should cry, Beware! Beware!
His twinkling eye, his thinning hair!
    Never join him on his spree
        And tip-toe silently to bed,
        For he on muffins hot hath fed,
And drunk some Horlicks for his tea.

N. J. WARBURTON

*

A Poem by Ronald Reagan, Non-poet

They say that love can never last. It really is a shame.
It's just a fact of nature, and I guess no one's to blame.
But since I've left my big white house in Washington, DC,
My life is like an empty road and people walk on me.

I used to be a lost black sheep in movie-making land,
Where reds and twangy-boys could earn an easy hundred grand,
But Jesus and the Cold War, gosh, they made me feel so swell,
I took off on the campaign trail to give those sinners hell.

I spoke the words they taught me, but the words don't mean a damn:
The public likes big helpings of its California ham.
My right hand played it one way while the left played it another,
But all the while the scoreboard flashed up NATION, GOD and
     MOTHER.

Now eight years is a winning streak — or so the Bible says —
And life is mighty cosy when you get to be the Pres.
But all good things come to an end: I felt it in my gorge
The day I packed my saddlebags and left it all to George.
It's grand to be with Nancy in our cabin in the West,
Where the blue Pacific stretches and the sun sinks down to rest.
But the sunsets all remind me that the best is not to be:
My life is like an empty road and people walk on me.

BASIL RANSOME-DAVIES

*

The Lake Isle of Innisfree
(The poet had now been in residence for some time)

I will arise and hoe now, and hoe on Innisfree –
  Though the bean cultivation has nearly got me paid!
Nine poultices in place now on stings of the honey-bee,
  It's dine on 'haricot hash, home-made'.

And I've got so much *grease* here, for grease comes dripping slow,
  Dropping from the bars of dripping, to where I'd put my things:
It soaks all through my jacket, and through my poet's-bow,
  It permeates to my shirts – AND CLINGS!

I will arise and hoe now, for always night and day
  I hear lake water seeping with low sounds through the floor;
As I do calculations to try and make it pay
  I find it all a *great big bore*!

P. I. FELL

*

The Rime of the Wedding Guest

Oh, what offence did I commit,
Dear Lord, that prompted Thee
To curse me with a mad old salt
Who bored the arse off me?

It was my kinsman's wedding day,
And gaily was I dressed,
When this seafarer's grubby hand
My well-groomed elbow pressed.

Though nuptial music filled the air,
Low did my spirit dip
As the grey dotard by my side
Intoned: 'There was a ship . . .'

Relentlessly he told his tale
About a voyage of woe;
A tale of tempest, storm and wreck,
Fierce heat and chill ice-floe.

240

A tale of dead men sailing ships,
Of crawlies in the deep,
Of every ill Fate could contrive
To make a man's flesh creep.

Disaster rained down blow on blow
Because (the old man swore)
He'd upped and shot an albatross –
A grave mistake, for sure!

The horrors he retailed at length
Impressed me less and less;
I simply grew to loathe his voice –
Its grinding awfulness.

At last, on a religious note,
He rounded off his tale.
Long was the wedding past; all drunk
The nuptial wine and ale.

God save all hardy mariners
Who brave the awesome sea:
But, when they spin such yarns as this,
Please keep them, Lord, from me.

PETER VEALE

*

If I should snuff it, sensitively say:
That there's some silent top-soil overseas
Shall still be solely Saxon. There shall stay
In that sweet sod a sweeter sod at ease;
A sod some Saxons spawned, schooled, sought to sow,
Sent out, snowdrops to smell, and streets to stride,
A Saxon stiff, sniffed Saxon breezes blow,
By streams sluiced, in its houses safe inside.

Sense this, the soul, its sins to simply cast
Aside, a sliver of the cosmic scheme,
Sends back the Saxon sentiments that blessed it:
Their shapes and sighs; their snooze that's seldom past;
And spoofs that schoolboys share; a soothing dream
For souls 'neath Saxon starscapes, surely rested.

BILL GREENWELL

*

W. S. GILBERT TRIES HIS HAND AT CHAUCER

**Extracts from the General Prologue to the Canterbury Tales.
Rewritten by Sir W. S. Gilbert**

The Prioress

PRI.   I am the very model of a medieval prioress,
My mind's refined and beautiful and so's each item of my dress.
My nasal intonation when I tackle any chant divine
Is very much admired and I am known as Madame
    Eglantine.
I only swear the gentlest oaths. My French is quite correct,
    although
I speak it like a native of the town of Stratford-atte-Bowe.
I've perfect table manners and no gravy on my bosom falls;
I never dip my fingers deep when dining in our cloistered halls.

ALL   She's perfect, etc.

PRI.   I'm very keen on etiquette, I practise it incessantly,
       I never grab or gobble and I'm always smiling pleasantly.
       I might have married royalty, I might have been a governess,
       But I'm the very model of a medieval prioress.

ALL   She might, etc.

PRI.   I ape the manners of the court, I feel obliged by my noblesse,
       I'm dignified and stately, but I'm also full of tenderness,
       For, oh, it does upset me if I see a little mouse entrapped,
       Particularly if it bleeds, or if its tiny neck is snapped.
       My charitable sympathies extend to these three hounds I lead:
       I feed them on the very best of roasted meat and milk and bread.
       If one of them should die, or any villain try to beat it up,
       I'd be in floods of tears but not leave grease on sorrow's bitter
          cup.

ALL   If one of them, etc.

PRI.   My brow is broad and handsome, it's a span almost of any
          hand,
       For I'm a woman stout and strong as any in this Engeland.
       This cloak I wear has quality and, so, unseen's, my hosiery,
       This clasp upon my arm is just a pretty little rosary –
       But don't the coral beads contrast most tastefully with
          those in green?
       And isn't this a lovely brooch in gold? You ask, what does it
          mean?
       Just possibly you're thinking that I'm stained by worldly
          vanity,
       So let me prove I'm guiltless of that secular inanity.

ALL   Just possibly, etc.

PRI.   It's my very private motto and it cures me of insomnia.
       It sums me up, you must agree: it's *Amor vincit omnia.*
       I might have married royalty, I might have been a
          governess,
       But I'm the very model of a medieval prioress.

ALL   She might, etc.

MONK Although, good friends, I am a monk
I've a belly like a woolsack,
I eat damned well and am often drunk
And I hunt my meat on horseback.
My stables teem with stallions fine
And the gay melodious jinglings
Of my bridles in the wind outshine
The chapel bell's loud ringings.

ALL   His bridles, etc.

MONK This chapel's at the convent where
I rule the roost. My habit
Is such that I am seldom there –
I'll never get to be abbot.
The tired old rule of Benedict
Would shackle us in the cloister,
Damns hunting and is far too strict –
It just isn't worth an oyster.

ALL   Damns hunting, etc.

MONK Why should I study and rack my brain
With a book at a library table?
Or weed the garden or clean the drain
When I could be down at the stable?
My dogs outpace the birds in flight
To bag the hares that feed me.
Let Augustine keep his books out of sight –
And that's my Nicean Creed, see!

ALL   Let Augustine, etc.

MONK I spend good money on my gear, dear sir,
As well as on going hunting.
My sleeves are trimmed with finest fur
And among my other bunting
Is a love-knot set in a golden pin
Which keeps my hood in place, sir,
So it can't fly off, which would be a sin,
When I'm riding in a race, sir.

ALL   So it can't, etc.

MONK   My pate is bald, my face is red,
       And glistens as if from oiling,
       My restless eyes glow in my head
       Like a furnace when lead is boiling.
       My boots are supple, I am no ghost,
       My horse is brown as a berry.
       I love a fat swan, and so, mine host,
       Let's eat, drink and be merry!

ALL   He loves etc.

MONK   For I am a monk.

ALL   And a good monk too!

MONK   And although I'm quite a hunk
       And you'll say my soul is sunk,
       None the less I am a monk.

ALL   And a good monk too!

MONK   I'm also a swell.

ALL   And a great swell too!

MONK   So that if I go to hell
       When they toll my funeral bell
       I should roast or fry quite well.

ALL   And we think so too!

The Wife of Bath

WIFE   As some day it may happen that a lover will appear,
            I've got a little list – I've got a little list
       Of my virtues and attractions for that worthy man to hear
            (I'm sexy, is the gist – I'm sexy, is the gist).
       The bad news first: I'm slightly deaf, a pity that, I know,
       But as weaver, I'm the tops and I can far outgo
       Those amateurs in Ypres and Ghent – I'm just as smart in church;
       If someone shoves in front of me I knock them off their perch;
       But the central fact about me is, I really must insist,
            I'm fond of being kissed – I'm fond of being kissed.

ALL   She's got a little list – she's got a little list;
       And she's fond of being kissed – she's fond of being
       kissed.

WIFE This drapery upon my head must weigh a good ten pound,
       It almost makes me list – it almost makes me list!
     My stockings – yes, you have a peep – are scarlet and
       renowned
       (They never should be missed – they never should be
       missed!)
     For I never let them wrinkle and I keep my shoes well
       shined.
     I'm very handsome looker, bold and florid but unlined:
     I've put myself about a bit and will while I'm alive;
     If they weren't dead you could enquire of any one of five –
     The husbands who came one by one to church and would
       insist
       I'm fond of being kissed – I'm fond of being kissed.

ALL   She's fond of being kissed – she's fond of being kissed;
       And it almost makes her list – it almost makes her list!

WIFE Of course, before I married them I loved some other chaps
       (I've got a longish list – I've got a longish list),
     But don't you be impertinent and dwell on those mishaps.
       Or you will feel my fist – I'll thump you with my fist.
     I've often been on pilgrimage – Jerusalem and Rome.
     Boulogne and Compostella and Galicia, Cologne.
     I've crossed a lot of Rubicons and wandered by the way,
     For I'm gap-toothed, lascivious, delight to lead astray,
     Such ardent fellow pilgrims as will join me in a tryst:
       I'm fond of being kissed – I'm fond of being kissed.

ALL   If she isn't being kissed – if she isn't being kissed –
       She will thump you with her fist – she'll thump you with
       her fist.

WIFE I scorn to ride side-saddle, for astride's the comfy way:
       I don't care if I'm hissed – I don't care if I'm hissed!
     My wimple's wide, my hat's a shield against the heat of
       day . . .
       Oh, laddie, grab my wrist – embrace me and enlist

In the battle of the sexes. I wear spurs to prod my mount,
This skirt conceals two hips like oaks whose strength is
paramount
In games of love, as you will find if you will only try.
I know it all – its remedies, manoeuvrings; that's why
I want you on this pilgrimage to be my catechist:
I so love being kissed – I so love being kissed.

ALL   She's put him on her list – she's put him on her list;
And quite soon he will be kissed – yes, very soundly
kissed!

TOM AITKEN

*

Rosencrantz and Guildenstern:
A Shakespeareanaddendum

KING   Thanks, Rosencrantz and gentle Guildenstern.

QUEEN   Thanks, Guildenstern and gentle Rosencrantz.

What if horrid plots are hatched?
We stand by. We are detached.
'Sitters-out at every dance' –
That is us, eh, Rosencrantz?

(*Refrain*)

Superfluity of gore
Is the rule at Elsinore!
Think of all one can discern
From the sidelines, Guildenstern.

Life's been more demanding since
Our involvement with the Prince!
'Form a view and take a stance?'
No, I think not, Rosencrantz.

247

We've had, when in troubled states,
Solace from our Laureates;
Listen: '. . . haunts of coot and hern' –
Rather good, that, Guildenstern?

P. I. FELL

A SPOT OF DEFLATION

DEFLATED COUPLETS

Whereby familiar lines of verse are given a new slant.

Myself when young did eagerly frequent
Houses of ill-repute — but not in Lent.

PETER VEALE

Drink to me only with thine eyes,
And spare the dwindling gin supplies.

MARY HOLTBY

When in disgrace with fortune and men's eyes,
The thing is to invent some thumping lies.

MARGARET MacINTYRE

When I consider how my light is spent,
I wonder where my box of matches went . . .

KATIE MALLETT

Stands the church clock at ten to three?
Does no one wind the thing but me?

MARTIN FAGG

Shall I compare thee to a summer's day?
You fit the bill – cold, dimmish, wet and grey.

MARTIN FAGG

A thing of beauty is a joy forever,
And sold, evades all Gains Tax, if you're clever.

MARTIN FAGG

Had I the heavens' embroidered cloths,
No doubt they'd soon be full of moths.

MARGARET MacINTYRE

To be or not to be, that is the question.
You see I'm always open to suggestion.

MARY HOLTBY

Thou still unravished bride of quietness,
Come to my bedroom quickly and undress.

MARY HOLTBY

Oh, my Love's like a red, red rose
Demolished by a garden hose.

MARTIN FAGG

Is this a dagger which I see before me?
Another pint of 'Strongbow' should restore me.

MARTIN FAGG

At last he rose, and twitch'd his mantle blue –
'Thank God!' he gasped, 'I found this *Portaloo*!'

MARTIN FAGG

Pale hands I loved beside the Shalimar,
A knocking-shop quite close to the Bazaar.

MARTIN FAGG

Ah, did you once see Shelley plain,
And is it true he had no brain?

MARTIN FAGG

She dwelt among the untrodden ways
And wore green wellies all her days.

MARGARET ROGERS

Come live with me and be my love:
Good heavens, drag *does* suit you, guv.

PETER VEALE

My true love hath my heart and I have his,
Such the state of organ transplants is.

V. ERNEST COX

Behold her single in the field:
Wait, the bowler has appealed!

JOYCE JOHNSON

Will no-one tell me what she sings?
'These are a few of my favourite things.'

GERARD BENSON

Should auld acquaintance be forgot?
Certainly not. Ask any Scot.

GERARD BENSON

Of Man's First Disobedience and the Fruit
I, personally, could not give a Hoot.

GERARD BENSON

Where are you going with your lovelocks flowing,
And your skirt hitched up and your knickers showing?

GERARD BENSON

Where the bee sucks, there suck I.
I don't feel well: I s'pose that's why.

N. J. WARBURTON

The Assyrian came down like a wolf on the fold,
A sight less than frequent in Stow-on-the-Wold.

TIM HOPKINS

A child should always say what's true.
A practice he will later rue.

TIM HOPKINS

The woods are lovely, dark and deep,
And I have Semtex to secrete.

TIM HOPKINS

Fair's foul and foul's fair
Until the action replay's on the air.

PETER VEALE

Once more unto the breach, dear friends, once more:
You're only friends until I've won the war.

NOEL PETTY

Yes, I remember Adlestrop;
The car park had a gifte shoppe.

NOEL PETTY

It is a beauteous evening, calm and free;
Let's get some chips and see what's on TV.

NOEL PETTY

Fear no more the heat o' the sun.
Use our cream and you won't get overdone.

N. J. WARBURTON

Farewell! thou art too dear for my possessing.
(We should have fixed the price before undressing.)

N. J. WARBURTON

She stood breast high amid the corn.
It took two days for her to mow the lawn.

N. J. WARBURTON

Uneasy lies the head that wears a crown;
Best take the darned thing off when bunking down.

MARGARET ROGERS

A sweet disorder in her dress.
That randy boss of hers again, I guess.

BASIL RANSOME-DAVIES

There was the sound of revelry by night,
And everyone was arseholed by first light.

BASIL RANSOME-DAVIES

They flee from me that sometime did me seek;
Methinks my after-shave is not so chic.

BASIL RANSOME-DAVIES

They fuck you up, your mum and dad,
And sex and work are just as bad.

REM BEL

Because I do not hope to turn again,
I have now moved into the right-hand lane.

REM BEL

To see a world in a grain of sand,
You have to be quite mad, or canned.

RON RUBIN

Jenny kissed me when we met.
I wish she'd buy a new Gillette.

RON RUBIN

I saw Eternity the other night.
It looked like Slough – or maybe I was tight.

RON RUBIN

O day and night, but this is wondrous strange –
The way they manage on the Stock Exchange!

PAUL GRIFFIN

A FEW FINAL WORDS

A Villanelle for Three Poets in Halley's Year, 1985

No more, when princes die, are comets seen,
Circling from distant realms beyond our ken;
A poet's verses keep his memory green.

We must not think the Heavens intervene,
To mark a human death with hydrogen;
No more, when princes die, are comets seen.

What lump of dirty ice, the stars between,
Does aught to honour human genius when
A poet's verses keep his memory green.

The solar wind is thin and cold and keen,
Who can suppose stars fall for mortal men?
No more, when princes die, are comets seen.

Graves, Grigson, Larkin, each in turn has been,
Delight always and genius now and then;
A poet's verses keep his memory green.

Three cool observers of our modern scene
Are gone; we may not see their like again.
No more, when princes die, are comets seen;
A poet's verses keep his memory green.

JOHN STANLEY SWEETMAN

Lament For The Minor Poet
(In appropriately blank, blank verse)

Behold this silent solitary fool
Who scratches here for themes and there for rhythms,
Submitting countless poems plus s.a.e.s,
Acquiring slips that endlessly regret;
No laurel crown for him, no glittering prize,
Through restless days and sleepless nights he toils
For scant reward, and if, against the odds,
His precious odes appear in print, he finds
Them skulking in the letters page or crammed
Inelegantly in the column-inch
Of space the editor was pleased to fill;
Yet still he scribbles on, sustained by dreams
Of future fame when light verse, fresh revived,
Finds public favour once again and his
Oft-failed MS, new-born in gilded boards,
Sells by the thousand and our 'Sunday Poet'
Will, in 'Tennysonian' splendour scale
The heights of Mount Parnassus, a feat
As likely as the sudden winged ascent
Of bristly ungulates (or common pigs).

PHILIP A. NICHOLSON

*

Death and the Poet

In your bereavement bear in mind
Such grief is common to mankind
And every poet worth his salt
Has mourned th' inexorable vault.
Where would our literature be
Had Lycidas not drowned at sea,
Or long-lived Hallam sadly missed
His laureate obituarist?

MARY HOLTBY

256

Bardic Lament

Why do we do it? Heaven knows –
We ought to stick to honest prose.
Mind you, Poetry's great to read;
It plugs a gap, fulfils a need,
And furthermore it's fun to write –
Oh, yes, Poetry's all right.
Then what's the catch? I hear you say.
The catch my friend? It doesn't pay:
Of all depressions nothing worse
Than getting back unwanted verse
With nothing more to meet your debts
Than unconvincing brief regrets,
And what is more some filthy beast
Returns it coffee-stained and creased;
Then, of course, you get the swine,
Like one who took some work of mine
Then published it (it took him ages)
Gratis in the letter pages.
Still, why go on; 'twas ever so,
The poet's sorry tale of woe.
And yet in spite of all we've learnt
Our fingers still are getting burnt.
Why persevere? As well ask why
A grounded bird attempts to fly.
Give it up while we draw breath?
No chance, the only cure is death.

PHILIP A. NICHOLSON

*

Final Cuplet

When I have fears that I will cease to be,
I go and make myself a cup of tea.

MARGARET ROGERS

*

Final Cuplet

When I have fears that I will cease to be,
I go and make myself a cup of tea.

MARGARET ROGERS

*

APPENDIX
The Devil's Glossary of Poetic Terms

Ambiguity A convenient domain for the poet to retreat to when he is not sure of his own meaning.

Anglo-Saxon An obsolete language which frequently surfaces during poetic discussion.

Argument What happens after the poetry reading.

Ars Poetica The poet's view of his beloved, in retrospect.

Bard No longer admitted to the Poetry Circle.

Beatitudes *Weltanschauung* of Allen Ginsberg & Co.

Blank Verse Writer's block.

Bouts Rimés Intermittent attempts at writing.

Bucolic Bookworm.

Burden Livelihood.

Burns Stanza Rejected MS.

Chain Verse Lyrics of blues originating in Southern US penitentiaries.

Cliché A handy device you would never use yourself.

Commercial (adj.) Making more money than you are.

Commission The sin of commission is the Eighth Deadly Sin.

Conceit One of several varieties of hubris the poet is prone to.

Concrete Poetry Poetry reading on the South Bank.

Corona Old-fashioned typewriter.

Critic 'A legless man who teaches others how to run.' (Now Barabbas was a critic . . .)

Cross Rhyme Generic name for the 1950s verse of the Angry Young Men.

Dialect (adj.) Incomprehensible.

Doggerel What other poets write.

Dramatic Monologue Poet's conversational style.

Enjambment The foot-in-the-door school of literary self-advancement.

Envelope Stanza Instalment of verse submitted to editor.

Eye Poetry Verse in the style of E. J. Thribb.

Fancy The poet's beloved.

Found Poem Juvenilia, which the poet hoped had been lost.

Fourteener Precocious young poet.

Free Verse Verse you wouldn't pay to hear.

Gnomic Verse Rhymes engraved upon the plinths of garden statuary.

Heptet The accompanying musical group at a jazz-and-poetry gig.

Heroic Line Heavy chat-up by the poet.

Hexameter Witches' incantation.

Hovering Accent An affliction common amongst actors when reading verse.

Imagism The poet's view of himself.

Inversion Homo-eroticism in verse.

Jingle One of the few financially rewarding avenues open to the poet.

Lai/Lay Poet's mistress.

Macaronic Verse School of poetry which originated in the polyglot eating-houses of Trieste.

Martian Poetry The picture-postcard school of verse.

Measure What the poet drinks before a reading.

Metre/Meter (US) What the critic (or editor) reads for a living when times are bad.

Middle English English, Home Counties style.

Mixed Metaphors A bad habit, almost as dangerous as mixing one's drinks.

Modern Movement Old-fashioned verse.

Muse Where the publisher lives.

Nonsense Verse Any verse you don't understand.

Objective Correlative The frank opinions of the poet's next-of-kin on his poetic efforts.

Occasional Poetry What a poet (or intellectual) reads between block-busters.

Octave The distance between a masculine rhyme and a feminine rhyme.

Outrageous Rhyme Filthy limericks.

Oxymoron Anyone who denigrates one's creative efforts.

Pathetic Fallacy The notion that money can be made from writing verse.

Plagiarism Homage.

Poesy The nosegay a poet sends his beloved.

Poet Laureate A sinecure you feel you could occupy more profitably than the present incumbent.

Poetic Licence An imaginary document which, if it existed, would be frequently endorsed.

Poetry Magazine Where the critics keep their ammunition.

Pure Poetry Poetry unsullied by sexual impropriety.

Rhyme Royal The verse style of Henry VIII.

Rime Riche Verse beloved of publishers.

Rising Foot A hazard to watch out for in publishers' offices.

Rude Rayling Generic term for Performance Poetry.

Saphhics Lesbian verse.

Secondary Accent Stage voice.

Silent Stress A complaint common amongst editors.

Singlet Garment popular at recitals of beat poetry in the 1960s.

Sound Poetry Well-constructed poetry. (Antonym: Unsound poetry.)

Tragic Irony A condition to which middle-aged poets are prone when they consider what they gave up in order to write.

Triad Chinese literary agency.

Tumbling Verse A school of poetry whose members originally met in an Earls Court launderette.

Verse de Société Courtly verse.

Waka Liverpool poet.

Weak Ending Non-climactic final couplet in the English or Shakespearean sonnet.

RON RUBIN

INDEX OF CONTRIBUTORS

INDEX